MW00625180

## To the reader

Thanks you for reading this document, the true essence of life lies in the freedom of thought, a power without limits that lies hidden inside every spirit, these are the first letters of the change in which humanity enters, an awakening of different consciousness, a vision among many that exist, a true art of mental power.

**Omar Hejeile Ch.**

**AUTHOR**
**Omar Hejeile Ch.**

Wicca editorial, rescue the immeasurable power of the human being and nature; a power that everybody has, feels, prescribes, but few know, through radio shows, encourage without imposing a truth or a concept, so that each one that feel the call from inside, who discovers the magic of dreams, and wants to get the knowledge, thus, the transformation of your life reaches the scepter **of happiness. The old religion has reborn... and is in your hands.**

# WICCA
## SCHOOL OF MAGIC

The old religion based in the magic knowledge of lost old cultures in time, escaped from the hyperborean world, reborn like the phoenix, the harmony of man with nature. Wicca, word that comes from Wise, Wizard, means *"The job of the wise" "The artisans of wisdom"*.

For millennia of persecution the old documents of the old religion remained hidden waiting for the propitious moment of rebirth, now, Wicca and Ophiuchus, recover some of the old knowledge of the lunar influx, the sun, the great Sabbats, the secret power of enchantments and spells, the art of sorceries, the infinite magic world of plants, the secret of the stars.

**More information about WICCA:**
**www.ofiuco.com**
**www.radiokronos.com**
**www.wiccausa.com**
**www.ophiuchus.us**

© **2019**

Author: **Omar Hejeile Ch**

All Rights Reserved

Title: Satanism, Wisdom for Initiates, A Spiritual Philosophy of Life

Original Title: Satanismo, Sabiduría para Iniciados,

Una Filosofía Espiritual de Vida - © 2018

ISBN 978-958-8391-35-9

Translated from Spanish by: The Global Institute of Languages and Culture, Inc.

SATANISM - ©2019

ISBN: 978-958-8391-38-0

Editorial Stamp: WICCA E.U. (978-958-8391)

ENCYCLOPEDIA: "Universo de la Magia"

Design and Layout: Mario Sánchez C.

No part of this publication, including the cover design, may be reproduced, stored or transmitted in any form or by any means, either electronically, chemical, mechanical, optical, recording, photocopying, nor television space, press, radio, internet without prior permission of the editor.

Based on the copyright the images used to recreate are of free use those that are inside the book.

www. ophiuchus.us

(Copyright 2019, All Rights Reserved EDITORIAL WICCA)

# SATANISM

## Wisdom for Initiates
## A Spiritual Philosophy of Life

# HA-SATAN

Nothing secret will remain that some day it will be not revealed, nothing exists that someday it'll not understood.

The time has come to open the door to the past, to go to the beginning of power by others used, it is time to awaken the latent sleeper, caught in the crypt of thought.

It is time, now, to wake up and to contemplate the reality of existence, it is time to allow god to die.

It is the hour of awakening to the new light of existence, being gods of life, being creators of tomorrow, being living gods, gods without temples or prayers.

Time has come to break the bonds, the reverence and the subjection, the time has come to awaken the sleeper, it is time to release the shackles liberating the hands of the chained ones, to abandon the supplications and the

prayers, the hope of a miracle, it is time to end forever with the bonds of reason, imposed in the endless interest of redemption.

A man of lies nailed to a cross, the redeemer, who charges for forgiveness, and pay for it, a man nailed to a cross, which many take as protection, but they do not see that he only remembers them that they are dead in their own cross.

Nailed their hands, because it prevents them from creating, working, caressing, subsisting, because their mental hands have been mutilated, thrown to the eternal fire.

But they are not the hands of those who condemn, kill, mutilate and destroy those who think differently, to those who used their hands to sow and cultivate, while others in manipulative prayers steal the bread, in tithing and alms, to enrich the coffers of a god of lies, who shouts "Mine is gold and silver, because I am a jealous and corrupt god".

To open the doors of time, to separate the darkness from the light, to delve into the recondite

depths, of a distant time, to navigate in the essence of life, the original labor of the creation.

On contemplating the existence, it is discovered that each body harbors a strange, different energy, an essence of immeasurable power, and the inner force of life, taking shape in the sense of the "BEING".

That mysterious force, acting with subtle changes of the rhythm of the lifetime, transforms itself between light and darkness, it advances in the same sense in everything when it exists, nothing dies that does not reborn, nothing increases that does not diminish, nothing flows that does not return to its origin.

The mind, in the same way has this characteristic of constant mutation, an eternal struggle for balance between two antagonistic forces, the distant and near extremes of freedom, good and evil.

To enter to the labyrinths of the freedom, arduous and difficult task, before such concepts, leads the being with the self-valuation of his actions moved by strange desires. Temptations or inspirations, auguries or predictions, encourage acting in one direction or another, concepts so dissimilar from those who judge them in the different circumstances of their view.

The infinite struggle between two stigmatized forces: one towards good, another towards evil.

So much is spoken about the good, that, in its eagerness to impose it, in the same way it is spoken more about the evil to fight it, doing of the good an evil worse than that one that is fought.

To enter the world of Satanism, is to enter the world of god, two extremes of freedom, representations darkness and light, good or evil, with all possible variants between one and the other one, up to the mysterious vortex of not finding where the one begins and where the other one ends.

About god, in his supposed good, much has been spoken, in fact, human existence in all its cultures, millions of gods representing good have been created by men, the infinite cosmos of religions with myriads of religious sects in adoration to each god, stone temples, colossal structures of incredible beauty, raised like altars to the sky in search of one or some, among all gods ... millions of them, millions cry them through prayers, supplications, petitions, imploring a blessing.

But, in spite of million and million of gods, there has existed **only one demon**, malignant representative of the night, Machiavellian and destructive, the alive and powerful evil, that even the infinite army of gods and angels have not been able to combat or minimize it, such is the power of the demon that every prayer to god, strengthens it, it is proclaimed that the good will end up by dominating the evil. Is it not that the god who is so much venerated is indeed the evil that weakens itself to be surrendered before a good that is considered as the evil?

How many churches and religions exist? How much gods fight among them, how many wars generated by imposing one over others, the war of beliefs, and a single demon, for which religions exist, if not for that single demon, unbeatable, uncontrollable, forbidden, master of the supposed evil, no god, no religion would exist.

This grimoire is not for the common people, the letters trapped in these pages will shake your spirit up to the beginning of time, it will take your mind to the labyrinth of doubt, disappointment, confusion, it will create illusory images in your thought, your soul will be transported in dreams to places that no human has been able to nor could imagine.

You will hear in your mind strange voices, you will be knowledgeable in secrets of power, visions will come, you will sense moments from the depths of your being, from the most intimate part of your traveler spirit of incarnations, the logbook of your experiences will be opened in the book of the wisdom.

This journey of your mind must be slow, meditated, you will enter into the sacred mysteries of the underworld, you will remove the veil of shadows, you will transit burning paths, and when ... your spirit has been squeezed, when your mind has approached the deepest of darknesses, maybe just maybe, you will find the maximum power of dominion, and I say maybe, because only the big ones, the strong of spirit, the rebels, ***those whom this book summons***, only they will know and will apply and will know the entire power of the freedom.

In the same way, as you progress in your reading, something from within your being will emerge to your consciousness, a voice, like a distant whisper will talk to you.

For others, the mentally dazzled, the useless ones, the incompetent, those who have succumbed in their spirit, it will be a book of infernal terror, for others, it will be only meaningless words and words.

Undoubtedly, voices will rise, critics will arrive, preachers of the good, the god's followers will shout heresy and blasphemy, they will rend their clothes, two in a bed will fight for this cause, the division will come, but ... nothing happens by chance, if your eyes read until the end, a second later, you will be free and you will dominate your world.

To start this process it is prudent to resort to a little magic, a way to unify with the energies that exist in the universe, before that, a small explanation, well, two explanations.

**The first**
This is not a book to read quickly or to anticipate the end, you will undoubtedly find attractive elements, beware, it is important to know each section and what it hides, to venture will be your responsibility, prudence dictates, go step by step.

**The second**
As this book is written, is based on a mysterious principle of unification, is slightly complex, but with a little attention you will understand it.

The whole knowledge of the universe is already caught in the some place of not time and space, we have heard about great geniuses, about great inventors, about great scientists, and, mostly, about curious and strange ways, they have found answers to big questions.

We call them initiates, geniuses, extremely gifted, all except Albert Einstein, (**He is a thief of ideas of his wife Mileva Maric**)

So it can be deduced that these people have been born with a predestined spirit, or marked with that wisdom.

I invite you to reflect about the following thing, your brain, is itself a chemical network full of neurotransmitters, identical in all humans, a neurologist identifies the same convolutions in all brains, but, the personality is different in each one.

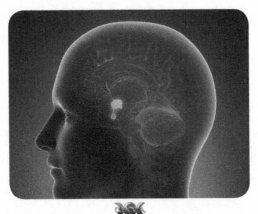

But, in the deepest of the brain a small gland exists with shape of the pineapple, the pineal gland, to not transcribe all his power, I invite you to read the first part of the book: **Conoce Tu Destino, Signos e Intersignos del Zodiaco [Know Your Destiny, Signs and Intersignes of the Zodiac].**

This gland has something special, I suggest you to keep in mind this section.

Now, wisdom or knowledge is not a mental factor, or association of information or inspiration, it is a certain vibration of everything that exists individually, let's say that Nikola Tesla, a genius of electricity, did he possess the implicit knowledge of it, or did he connect with the wisdom of electricity?

Who knows more about electricity than the same electricity, if he, in his meditation moments did not develop mental calculations, but, psychically he joined with the essence of his desire, feeling the vibration, transforming it into inspiration that, in turn, becomes codified impulses for the brain and therefore in thoughts. As he said, he got inspiration (As a comment, Tesla was born under a strong storm of lightning and thunders).

The universe is full of infinite wisdom, not within reach of a few, but of all, an unlimited flow of energy combinations, wave frequencies perceptible in states of relaxation, no physical vibrations that are received by the pineal gland.

It may sound crazy, but you can check it, in ancient Greece there was an old philosophical art, the ***"Maieutics"*** the art of giving knowledge, answers, from inside of each one.

Endeed it's about leaving the mind serene allowing it to flow inwards, doing so it connects with what you want, at the beginning it is vague, empty, parasitic thoughts block the flow, but, if you slowly deepen, you will perceiving that in your mind they appear as memories, information that you don't know why you know it, and, if you try to talk about that theme, without giving priority to your will, without thinking about what you say, but flowing with what you say, you will be surprised how much you know, without knowing it.

Who is energetically connected with a certain knowledge, he does not learn it, the knowledge flows from his inner, it is perhaps the reason why, certain people join with certain vibrations that finally do not correspond with academic learning, or they show a great facility for some knowledge.

Taking in account the previous thing, being a hypothesis, (later you will realize) if in the universe there is the whole knowledge, what will happen when it flows in the wisdom of freedom?

Did you had presentiments? On having discovered a theme related to your life, without prior knowledge, how do you know that you know it?

To enter to this treatise, it is important to join with the darkness, Satan is hidden there.

The moon has a strange influence, denied, accepted, assumed, proven, each according to their concepts, as well as their knowledge about the theme concludes with which it is identified.

## Ritual opening the grimoire

A monk in a temple lights incense and enters into deep meditation, a scientist lights a cigarette, an architect contemplates emptiness, a critic condemns what he can not do and although he wanted he does not have with what, a lawyer walking in circles looking for answers.

All somehow perform actions to awaken their Maieutics, they perform a ritual where the mind enters beyond the thoughts.

A man or a woman before an appointment groom their hair, they look for the best suits, they perfume their body, they prepare themselves, who is going to graduate does the same, who is going to start a trip, all someway perform a series of rituals to open the doors of future, similarly, to enter this universe, you must be prepared.

### *For this ritual is requested:*
• A hood, something that covers your face and hides it
• Two candles, one black and one white
• A chalk or lime, to trace a pentagram and a circle in which you may be standing or sitting
• A stone or rock that must accompany you during the reading

- A cup with water, which you can drink
- Incense

Now you must wait for a full moon night, your intuition will tell you when you should be internally prepared for this step. To read the book for reading it is a good option, before performing a ritual that undoubtedly will change your life.

### Full Moon Night six in the afternoon

Sunset time, when the day merges with the night, it is the time to prepare the altar.

It is necessary with advance to have looked for an external place, farm, terrace, park, a solitary place, where there is no danger, to realize the opening, if you say: that is difficult or I cannot, put away the book, it is not for you.

It requires a series of steps, demanding you to perform acts for which you must find solutions, strategy, look at how you can perform them, that is start entering in the power of your inner.

## *Ritual*

Now, an interesting part of your life comes, if this grimoire has come into your life, it is because something in your restless spirit has shown you another path... to enter the knowledge of your inner world it is time to renounce the knowledge of the external world.

It is time to communicate with the cosmic vibration of wisdom.

## *To renounce*

Creeds, dogmas, paradigms, you have been trained to think about being follower and not leader, to be one more among the common, not different, you have been trained since childhood, to believe not to know.

You has been submitted to rituals that limit your free essence, you has been invaded by mental brakes, sin, negation, limitation, you has been induced that while more miserable you are, better your spirit will be, not in this life but in the other, you have been mentally stoned.

Despite the power implicit in your essence of life, your mind is which prevents you from being, and this is due to the amount of information and mental training you have received, how many times have you knelt down crying out, asking, requesting, instead of getting up to act?

It's time to be free ... this ritual is a pact between you and the power of your essence ...

 Start by drawing a large circle, inside it design a reverse five-pointed star, it results a triangle below and two above, as shown in the image.

Later you will understand the meaning of this symbol.

Being inside, place on your right side the white candle, on your left side the black candle, the cup with water between the two points, from above, the rock at the bottom point.

In the middle, the two incenses, when the moon begins to light, take off the shoes, cover your head, you can sit or stand, concentrate on the next decree ... but think, imagine, and be aware of your desire.

Light everything … candles and incense …
Say:

*I* (say your name)
*Today, under this full moon, witness*
*of the passage of time*
*Today, on this date without date.*
*Today I renounce to all beliefs about spirituality*
*Today, I stop praising a god or worshiping a demon*
*Today I renounce a baptism imposed*
*and unwanted*
*Today I renounce the mental submission*
*of religions*
*Today I renounce the symbols that submit*
*mind and soul*
*Today I renounce the crucified ones who*
*call themselves teachers*
*Today I renounce the hypocrisy of*
*sellers of faith*
*Today I renounce being a slave and submitted*
*Today I renounce god and his angelic court,*
*I renounce the imposed truths,*
*Today, I renounce being a slave of other*
*thoughts*

*Today, I renounce expect a prize or*
*a punishment*
*Today, I renounce my past.*

*I renounce god, the demon, all*
*the imposed beliefs, I renounce with the*
*predestined, I renounce to believe, with this*
*renunciation, I leave clear, that now ...*
*I will advance on the path of knowledge.*

*Today I agree to enter the world of*
*freedom of thought, without stereotypes,*
*without mental conductions, without prescripts framed*
*in good and evil,*
*Today I am free, I will be god and demon,*
*the sole creator of my destiny.*

*This is my pact, as a witness*
*I leave the night, which will open the day of my*
*illumination, I drink the enchanted water, to cleanse all*
*the rituals, which were*
*imposed to me, I erase from my soul a*
*baptism of slavery, I erase from my soul*
*a piece of bread, with which they submit the*

*conscience, in a host of forgiveness of
a not realized sin.*

*With this water,* (take the cup and drink)
*I purify myself in my own baptism
of cleanliness and freedom,
I unite with the eternal wisdom,
I unite myself, with the total power of life,
I unite with the incredible strength of existence that flows
through me …*

*In this stone … I bury forever,
the redemption of the weak ones, the path for
me, in my chosen freedom, is the path of
wisdom.*

Finished with the above, use the stone as an element of accompaniment and remember while you read this grimoire, meditate a little on your life, on your actions, now with that hood close your life to the outside world, think, in full wisdom, in the wealth you want, the health you miss, the love you wish, everything, when your mind can imagine and desire, is latent in your inner strength, **renounce everything, to have everything.**

The human being, regardless of gender, possesses in his interior a fantastic and powerful spirit, which flows through the mind, which in turn is programmed by culture, education, traditions, dogmas, motivations and limitations.

All beings from the beginning, prior the conception are free, competitive, fighters, brave and strategists. There is no spirit, or being that comes into the world with a sin, that is, a submitted defeatist.

When observing the genesis of each being, it is understood that at the fertilization moment a cruel battle begins for the gestation of an ovule ... million spermatozoids begin a competition of obstacles and difficulties, among two hundred and fifty million and a billion of spermatozoids, compete, each with a different spirit, they fight a pitched battle, all impelled by the force of the life, they look for the end: the ovule.

There is no one single that is a weak or defeated, or sinner, they all are winners, and a different spirit impels them all.

Have you ever thought, that the siblings, being children from the same father, from the same mother, with genetically equal bodies, they have different spirits, each spermatozoon is a single spirit, a distinct personality, a different being.

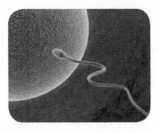

Since that time, one competes stronger, faster, one wants to be the first one and the **ONLY ONE.**

And the winner, the best, **IS YOU** ... that's why you're here, reading these lines. The day your father ejaculated inside your mother's womb, approximately two billion spermatozoids competed to fertilize the ovule, only one, the best was the winner, you, my friend, since you are in this world you are already a winner.

**A power pact is not made with a weak and poor mind...**

All beings possess that force, to be happy, to achieve

goals, to save obstacles, to get fortune, to achieve their dreams, to obtain love, passions, to enjoy the success, to turn dreams into reality, to live the experience of life to the fullest.

But, god does not allow it; he takes away the opportunity, while Satan gives you absolute and total **FREEDOM.**

**Free spirits... without limitations...**
**This is the entrance to the true hell of power, you can still renounce and die crucified, in the human stupidity, or liberate your soul and conquer life.**

Before starting, it is important to clarify some concepts, you will start a mental journey through time, you will immerse yourself in the world of darkness, with all the elements that this entails, in fact you will enter to the same hell.

The veil of your mind will break; you will discover the entire power of the freedom of your spirit's freedom by understanding and discovering your incredible and implicit abilities, you will understand that you are definitely more than a simple human being, you are the real power made flesh. But for this you must relearn the sacred value of life.

Very rarely, adventurers of thought dared to face the rules, dogmas, creeds, entering the labyrinths of the hidden and infernal power of wisdom.

In this moment you receive the invitation to enter into the depths of the antithesis of all beliefs.

You are free to continue or to stop, I must clarify that the content of this grimoire, is for freethinkers, evolved beings clamoring for an awakening, beings whose restless spirits shout them in the silence of thought that there is something more, that there is another view of the mystery and magic, somewhere in your essence, a truth is hidden, maybe these pages are one of many answers.

The universal truth, does not exist, the reality of the truth is that one that everyone, under a logical, honest, sincere analysis, discovers in his inner and considers that it is his truth.

# SATAN

"To define a name, it is complex, to define a being for a name, it is still more complex, to define the indefinable, by a name or a being, is to find the wisdom". O.H.

**Who is Satan?**
**What would you respond to this malignant question?**

Thousands of responses stand out, probably a worry appears in the mind, they emerge the memories of preconceived fears, and maybe you will cross yourself as protection to the unknown.

*"I am going to accompany you in this adventure of the spirit, I will speak to you as if I was next to you. In fact, I will be interrogating you, you will realize with surprise how much you know."*

**Let's think**

For a moment, I am going to invite you to reflect, for thousands of years, it has sought to fight a demon, wars, killings, destruction, every second someone screams; that evil must be combated, and evil ultimately covers everything.

So that evil, must be a creation bigger than the good that created it, taking into account that the creation that created evil could not fight it.

It must be an infinite evil, with an infinite wisdom. You imagine how much strategy it must use, up to the point of doing good, to get followers who follow a good, without knowing that it comes from evil.

But it would be that evil, that has generated the biggest conflicts of humanity, is contemptuously, named only thirty-three times in the Old Testament, in the book that has submitted, enslaved, and destroyed million human beings?

Is that, the birth of the demon of evil, and so scarce its presence in one of the sacred books?

In ancient Hebrew, the word Satan, Satan, does not relate to a being as such, it is something deeper, it represents the opposition, the enemy, the executioner, the force of the reason **"THE ADVERSARY"**

Is it possible to think that such an infinite evil is so little recognized? Or is so scarce, as void, the wisdom of that evil?

We must think that behind the dogmatic concept of Satan, there is something that is infinitely powerful, extremely dangerous, which is intended be kept secret for all eternity.

But this concept, takes shape in the energy of each being that knows his profound essence.

Thus, a concept, a knowledge, a philosophy, an art, becomes a being, humanizes power, transforming it into a cruel, frightening, destructive monster, moving away for fear any proximity to its profound essence.

But, it is a being, with a different philosophy, an unlimited power, a force so powerful that dominates even his creator, a power devoted to a few.

Religion, has imposed a basic dogma of all its wealth, fighting not Satan or what it represents, but to destroy the wisdom of evil, the wisdom of freedom of thought, to destroy completely its essence.

If men were wise, he would understand the moral poverty and ignorance of religions, freeing himself from the slavery of the god's dogma, but the astute religion suggests, imposes, submits through selective assassination, which must prevail "fear to god" and every wise person will die as a heretic, burned or stoned and obviously, wisdom can not come from evil.

Although, for thousands years, god the omnipotent one, could not destroy it, if he, that everything knows and created everything, did not do it, could not, he was not able to, how his ignorant serfs will do it?

Very simple the response, it is not a physical being that is pursued, it is the knowledge of an unlimited power that one wishes to fight through the fears rooted in the psyche of those blind and stupid who appeal to god to save their souls.

Preys easy to indoctrinate, the religion creates the demons, but he could never fight them and neither it is interested in, without demons there is no business.

But easy, in the same bible Salomon the most wise man of the world, it was easy for him to take names of other gods and to create the followers of the devil, today it is easy to find themes like the Demonology, another ridiculous brainwashing eyesore. In the case that demons existed who damn did put them not human beings names? Simple, the human beings …

**Satan** is the power, the total force as creative essence, is the wisdom made flesh. But condemned, limited, submitted, to be the element that allows in its existence, the proliferation of gods and religions, all fighting evil, and fighting among themselves.

Thousands of incapable gods, millions of priests sick of deep aberrations, likewise, if god could not, much less them.

**It is no wonder that they charge much money tithes with the story of fighting evil, that in the end, the evil that is fought, is the same or worse than that one, which is used to combat it.**

In other words, an evil disguised as well is used, to fight the evil. Now, a bit of history, the star with a weak light, to be seen, requires the darkest night.

…Where an unlimited power can hide and be hidden, rather than inside the evil, who would dare to enter to the domains of the evil, to discover it?…

# BEGINNING OF SATANISM

Every tree, every star, every galaxy, all knowledge, all history, all life, all existence, has a root, a genesis or beginning, the same demon and same god, have a beginning.

Satan is not different, sometime it had its genesis, a series of events ignored by everyone even by the same religion; this ignorance gave way to the legends, comments, stories, suppositions that move the mind away from reality by immersing it in fantasy.

For years it has been hidden for the common, delving into the endless history of the times, we are going to enter the infernal labyrinth, to find the birth of Satan.

When riding on the wind of time to the past, paying the sacred pence of Charon nothing better than entering the confines of the underworld, where darkness opens the door of the infernal world, and in it, the history of Satan.

**Sumer**

Observe very well the following image

# PAZUZU

In life learning, nothing better than to go to the root of what you want to know, and for that, let's go to the essence of Satanism.

Let's look at the strange birth and interesting birth of Satan.

In ancient Sumer, someone, six thousand seven hundred  years ago, as you read it, 6,700, years, 4,700 B.C. took the trouble to carve this strange figure, which gave life to what is today known as Satan, Satanás and Satanism.

This figure is  located at the Louvre Museum.

Let's do a bit of I.R.I. (Interpretative Reverse Engineering)

Who, how, why, for what, did design so strange image?
What was its initial meaning?
Whom does it represent?
What did he do to be revered?

What is the reason, for this object to exist? Someone must have known him, express him, to do a carving, to create an idol, which has a series of meanings, lost forever, leaving only the sample of its existence.

It doesn't exist, a metalsmith that can create an image, symbol, icon of something that he has not seen... no one can imagine something he doesn't know.

Could you imagine a Xendra?
But … it was not only in Sumer where so strange being appeared … let's do a tour.

## Ecuador

Now, even stranger, in the South American continent, the Shuar people in Ecuador, there was an extraordinary encounter for the same epoch or closely in time, no kind of communication between Sumer and Shuar is intuited. And much less due to the colossal distance at that time.

("A Xendra is a transparent plane, a crystal bubble, similar to a soap bubble in which one can travel. (Extraterrestrial spacecraft) now, with this information, your mind can imagine.")

To the south of Ecuador, hidden inside the thickness of the forest, there is the Tayos cave nest of small nocturnal birds called Tayos or nightingales.

A little information, five to seven thousand years ago, it occurred to someone leave a strange riddle to archaeologists of future, buried in the Tayos cave.

The following images are a vision of this extraordinary place.

Magical place with incredible beauty, for a moment imagine this place 7000 years ago.

And what does this have to do with Satan? You will already know it ...

Well, inside this cave or door of another underworld, some suggestive objects were found. And some allude to something already seen.

And for your surprise I invite you to observe the following figure with whole concentration and attention.

Some gold tablets, found in the Tayos' cave in Ecuador.

Undoubtedly, the reader is invited to do an investigation on this incredible and unknown event.

...Now, well, taking this information and, without imposing a truth, the original source of a "Being" that would later become Satan has its origin in knowledge, a different philosophy lost in time.

How, Shuar people revered at the same being, and sculpted his presence or how the Sumerians lived in Ecuador?

In the ruins of the Tayos cave, this engraving was found on a gold sheet. Who did it, whom did it revere?

Looking at the two figures, one of profile another in front is easy to recognize its resemblance, the crests, the wings and the body language, which suggests some kind of implicit information.

Two cultures separated by time and space, with a common influence, something strange there is behind this event, but everything doesn't end there.

## Greece

Two thousand years ago B.C. or four thousand since the date, approximately 2,700, after the existence of the Sumerians, Greece is created, a strange, magical highly cultured world, cradle of legends and great thinkers.

And there, another part of Satanism is born, as a philosophy and as being.

## The God Pan

 Father of pantheism, with a very interesting concept repudiated and condemned by the church referring to the view, that god or the creator and creation, are the same, in other words, god in everything, everything in god, this way any being, no matter what it

is, is god, and god, not as an entity or humanized energy, he is in everything created.

Not as an individual, external, unattainable being, the pantheism suggests an inner energy implicit in everything, and all essence of that energy, everything is god. Or better, everything is energy, and everything is in that energy and the energy is in everything.

The god Pan, also known as Faun, is considered the son of Hermes the messenger of gods, Pan, half human - half male goat, had great powers, sexuality, enchantment, owner of fertility, creator of satyrs and nymphs, he had a syringe or flute with which acted on the harvests, life and sex.

But, more deeply, he exposed the philosophy of his father, the god Hermes. Philosophy that later the church would try to make fun of it, making Pan something burlesque, transforming it into the living image of the devil, annulling this way, the deep knowledge.

And by the way, generating terror on the Faun universe, Pan, represents the entire freedom, the secret power, the force, the rebellion, the anarchy, from there the name of panic is born, as an element of subjection, the church distorts the reality, destroys old documents, it appropriates knowledge, turning it into evil.

Male goat, Satan representation in the different coven, just as in the meetings that were realized in the covens. (Aquelarre, place where the goats graze, used to realize a Coven)

Pan = All
Teos = God. Pantheism, everything is god, god is everything.

## Europe

For the same date between 7,000 and 6,400 years in Northern Europe, the appearance of the Hyperborean ones, the beginning of the Celtic culture, the dynamic force of life, the power and knowledge of the magical events of the alteration of nature, through mental processes.

Really nobody knows who were or from where they came form, like other groups, their presence has been a mystery, there are some traces, which allow deducing their great knowledge, along with the ability to alter the material world, an unknown power.

## The Celts

## God Cernunnos

Or beings of the shadows, hidden people, children of darkness, travelers of the night, they were identified, with the world of mystery, they dedicated their time to the study of occult sciences, mainly

 based on a lunisolar calendar with which they performed portents, influencing on harvests, fertility, they have been recognized for their secret powers, knowledge imparted by the druids or Celtic priests, great magicians and witches full of wisdom.

With them the old religion is born, today known as **Wicca,** which means **"The craft of the wise"**

It is from the druids the appearance of the male goat, again. With a strange symbolic association with another figures found in the Tayos' cave in Ecuador.

**Gundestrup Cauldron**
The Holy Grail?

## Cernunnos

Antlered Celtic god, a magical power, the male goat of nature.

(Musée du Moyen-Âge at Cluny, Paris Archeological Museum,

Saint-Germain-en-Laye)

## Egypt

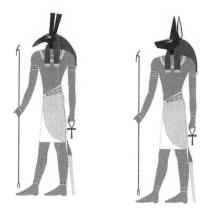

God Seth and god Anubis, owners of death and the underworld.

## Sumerian God Ningishzida

Sumerian God, Father Mother of Pazuzu and of all the gods and demons, interesting similarity between the Sumerian god and that found in Ecuador.

In this small tour, we find that some kind of extraordinary event happened around the world, these are some of the most relevant examples, but some similar is found in Chinese, Maya culture, etc., it is somewhat difficult to suggest that these cultures obtained a similar knowledge only based on legends, in such remote times when their existence was ignored by everybody...

...or not? It is a theme that remains open for your restless spirit, investigate a little.

The church, expert somehow of this type of event, begins a total persecution against all kinds of thought different from the concept of monotheism or a single god, it imposes its terrible and merciless law, injecting in mind the concept of the biblical god, a bloodthirsty and destructive being.

For a thousand years, between 476 and 1453, the church instituted obscurantism, the brainwashing of the generations, it tried to erase all traces of past knowledge, it submitted the world to ignorance, which unfortunately today remains.

The persecution to witches, magicians, sorcerers, it was the worst act of barbarity of humankind, it has been the church, in its aberrant thinking, which devised the worst torture a man can inflict on a woman and another man, the most atrocious pain *"honor and respect for those who died this way"*.

Torture created by the damn Inquisition and all its entourage of assassins, supposedly looking for Satan.

The iron maiden      The pear, anal
and vaginal

The ripper of breasts      The turtle of death

They are many, this is only a sample of the brutality, the way in which the church tried to silence any concept, thought or act related to the freedom.

...These legends, misrepresented, were associated with evil, hell, sin, in this way, the knowledge of Satanism, was associated with the infernal, the satanic and demonic concept, thus the church obtained for itself the "power" creating the subjection.

Everything bad, perverse, evil and sin, was attributed to the shepherd, the peasant known like pagan, strange relationship that the church associates with flock, the pastor of souls, the papal crozier or ferula, even in the churches sing "You are my pastor, I shall not want", etc. Just to think.

Basically, these cultures gave life to the origin of Satanism, however, is related to the same theme, and with other gods considered by the church like demons, belonging to the kingdom of hell.

In current era, after years of ignorance and beliefs in hell and devil, allowing the incalculable enrichment of the church, thanks to the sale of Satan as the malefic, a new crusade begins, Satanism, trying to mix and merge a number of issues, showing that evil, as such, does not exist, the church in spite of its persecution and killings, failed to extinguish the flame of freedom of spirits.

*The restart of Satanism has not been easy.*

Millions of Catholics, politicians, supposed and big theologians, professors, universities, scientists, researchers, believers, impose in the generations the same divine paradigm of god, the same stereotype, the same history, the same concept, annulling human freedom.

Like the previous, looking for the grammatical origin of the name with which today Satan is identified ... let's look at history ... the beginning of modern Satanism, far from the old philosophies and fantastic beings.

# BAPHOMET

Androgynous, Doctor: Heinrich Khunrath

# BAPHOMET
## KNIGHTS TEMPLARS' GOD

Baphomet of Eliphas Lévi

**Baphomet**, originally, without the Sumerian philosophies and from other places of the world, including Pazuzu, it appears in the comments of Dr. **Heinrich Khunrath**, (c. 1560 - September 9, 1605) physician, esoteric, eccentric character, disciple of the teachings of the great Alchemist **Theophrastus Phillippus Aureolus Bombastus von Hohenheim** (November 1493, September 24,1541), known such as Paracelsus

...According to Eliphas Lévi says in his book, "the Baphomet of the Templars, is a name that should be read cabalistically in reverse, and is composed of three abbreviations TEM OHP AB, Templi omnium hominum pacis abbas, father of the temple, universal peace of men; the Baphomet was, according to some, a monstrous head; according to others, a demon in the form of a male goat. Recently it was disinterred a sculpted coffer from the ruins of an ancient temple, and the antiquarians observed in it a baphometic figure, according to the attributes, to our male goat of Méndez and to the androgynous of Khunrath. This figure is bearded, with a woman's entire body; it has the Sun in one hand and the Moon in another, tied to chains. It is a beautiful allegory that this virile head attributes only to the thought the beginning and creative principle"

The influence of these characters, influenced directly on the psyche of Eliphas Lévi who for that time in which he belonged to the society of fog, where Jules Verne the great seer, knew the art of living eternally, a series of interesting events on this ancient knowledge.

...Among all the possible meanings of the origin, though, somehow they are related, that of greater acceptance, is that means "***Baptism of Wisdom***" the combination of two Greek words; Baphe Metis, in another translation "***Initiation by Baptism***"

This is deducted, taking into account that the most ancient texts belonged to the Greek language. But there is more...

## Mandaeans

In the whole region of Mesopotamia, where Sumerian  people lived, those who initiated the culture and the civilization, there is the Jordan River, there, in antiquity lived the Mandaeans sect, today almost extinct, the gnostic or wise people, also known as the nazir or nazarites, the pure ones who practiced, and even today, the ritual of baptism in the Jordan is practiced, as an initiation to wisdom. (***See the book Viaje al Apocalipsis - Travel to the Apocalypse***).

Thus, the nazir, nazirites performed the nazireate, water ritual for those consecrated to god. The same baptism of religion. This historical relationship broadly for not to transcribe all the information and to invite the restless spirits to investigate, shows us that Baphomet has its origin in the old Mandeans ritual of the gnostic or wise people, the Nazireate, but not as consecration to god, since as the awakening of consciousness and wisdom.

In fact, from Mandaeans the commandments are born. And it is not difficult to associate the history arranged of John the Baptist.

## Mandaeans Mandates

1. Do not blaspheme.
2. Do not murder.
3. Refrain from all adultery.
4. Do not steal.
5. Do not lie.
6. Do not give false testimony.
7. Refrain from disloyalty and dishonesty.
8. Refrain from all lust.
9. Do not practice magic and sorcery.
10. Do not get circumcised.
11. Refrain from alcoholic beverages.
12. Do not practice usury.
13. Do not mourn death.

14. Do not eat dead animals, pregnant or attacked by other furious animals or blood.

15. Do not to get divorced (except in exceptional cases).

16. Do not to commit suicide or abort.

17. Do not auto torture or practice abstinence.

Millenniums have elapsed since the first texts were found, and obviously the church was in charge of arranging things for its purposes, among them to impose the baptism, not like an initiation of ancient knowledge, but as a symbol of subjection, and undoubtedly accommodating the mandates.

Observing the different events exposed, intertwining events, knowledge from such great thinkers, (**Honor them**) a series of questions highlight.

# THE CHURCH AND ARMY OF GOD

Since we are talking about the same devil, it is appropriate venting the hypocrisy of the church, the mental and physical misery into which it has subjected humanity through a series of distorted dogmas, keeping away all beings from the true wisdom, where equality and equity are the progress of the nations.

Let's see, as both Levi and the other authors of Baphomet, let see the roots of the different cults and rituals executed by the Church, by stealing the philosophy and knowledge of the pagans, or PANTHEISTS.

The admirers of the male goat, for not to transcribe the whole story, I invite the reader to read the book ***RITUALES SECRETOS DE MAGIA Y BRUJERÍA*** [***Secret Rituals of Magic and Sorcery***].

Let's see something interesting, this story has its origin in the adoration of the god Pan and Baphomet, by almost no one, the Templars, the bloody and armed arm of the church.

**Who were the Templars?**

 **The Order of the Poor Companions of Christ and of the Temple of Solomon, also called the Order of the Temple, the Knights Templars.**

Nine men led by Hugues de Payns, founded between 1118 and 1119, the largest army of the military and Christian orders.

But the reality is different, a horde of barbarians, savages, assassins, ruthless, rapists and thieves who protected by the church and under the pretext of protecting pilgrims and cities supposedly "sacred" where the church imposed its creed, stolen from others cultures.

They dedicated themselves to kill, to plunder, to rape; women, children, elders, they instituted the BUSINESS OF THE CHURCH, the finances, the first banks, as well as they controlled all trade in the Middle East, some real thugs and killers, all in the name of God.

They were dedicated only to kill in the damn crusades imposing by blood and sword the religion that today many people follow in their spiritual blindness.

The first crusade and perhaps most important, it was on July 15, 1099, they conquered the city of Jerusalem, founding the Kingdom of Jerusalem, no one could ever imagine barbarism, the massacre committed with such ferocity in this crusade, which really threw a message of terror. Now, if you hear the news from the Middle East you could understand a little more where the problem was born, it was not only to impose a religion but it was to appropriate the wealth and the navigation of the Mediterranean. (I invite you to read and to investigate)

Like example this one is the map of the theft of the church in the crusades A TOTAL BUSINESS.

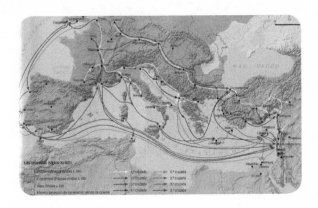

For two centuries the bandits dominated, up to the point that the church got scared and, because it could not leave loose ends, the Templars ruled everything, wealth, towns, cities, navigation, at any time, they would end up with the same church. Something that undoubtedly they should have done. But the brainwashing could more in some.

In the year 1307 to 1314 the church started another barbarity like to torture, to burn, to kill and to destroy its armed arm, in 1312, Pope Clement V ended up with the order of the Templars, but church stayed with everything, well almost all, because some Templars escaped with a great wealth.

The church had plan b, already created, it destroyed the Templars, but trained another worse bloodthirsty group, another horde of assassins.

The damn Inquisition, founded in the year 1184, in this way, what the Crusades not finished, now they would do it, and for that, nothing better than to persecute all those who were not paying tithes or were kneeling down.

Thus the Church pay well serves to whom serves it, there is a curse of the Templars, when they were burned, Pope Clement V was the first, then the King, and well some more popes are damned ... in fact the Templars cursed the church someday they will destroy themselves.

It happens that the power of the Templars was not given by god, they adored the male goat, they learned the arts of the old religion, they knew the secret powers of wizards and witches, that was the reason why the church murdered them, many were saved and around there big treasures are hidden. A thief who robs a thief…

Pope Sylvester II, with the faun … or the demon?

The genesis of the Bible, is nothing more than a robbery, a plagiarism, a cheap transcription of the genesis of the Sumerian history, I invite the reader to scrutinize, to read, to investigate, and to extract his own conclusions.

# BAPHOMET

Baphe Métis, **"Initiation by Water"**

Undoubtedly, the existence of a great man, **Alphonse Louis Constant**, later known as Eliphas Levi, a magician,

priest, writer, occultist, who gave life to the current Baphomet, must be ventilated. More due to the influence of other writers than by the appearance of his different representations in the world, these influences in the life of Eliphas Levi, allowed him to relate the male goat of Méndez, the maximum power of the Templars, with Pazuzu, but ignoring the deep philosophy there hidden.

From his room, when he wrote the book, ***Dogme et rituel de haute magie.***

In which, he relates the power of the male goat; bastion of the Templars, in this section the current Satanism is born.

# Section of the book.

"ADAM, and on other one that of EVE, and then those of AZOE and INRI, on the other two sides. At the head of a French translation of a book of Mr. of Nuisement, about philosophical salt, one can see the spirit of the earth standing on a cube, traversing tongues of fire; it has as phallus a caduceus, and the sun and the moon on the chest, to the right and to the left; it is bearded, it is crowned and has a scepter in the hand. It is the azote of the wise people on a salt and sulfur pedestal. Placing sometimes at this picture the symbolic head of the male goat of Méndez; it is the **Baphomet of the Templars,** the male goat of the Sabbath and the created verb of the Gnostics;"

He was the founder of the Sociedad de la Niebla [Mist Society], along with Julio Verne, Alexander Dumas father, Alexander Dumas son, through various rituals, each separately found a way to hide great knowledge.

I invite the reader to investigate in the book La Dama de las Camelias [The Lady of the Camellias], there are many magical secrets.

The Baphomet of Eliphas Levi is born from the combination of the influence received, in his priestly education, together with the influence of the thought of other writers.

He does not mix the old philosophies, or Pazuzu or the other ancient symbols, these symbols inspired the gargoyles of the Cathedral of Notre Dame, as well as the church of Saint Merry, these gargoyles inspired Levi.

Somehow indirectly the old images influenced the mind of this great magician.

Ironically, these two churches are the mothers of modern Satanism.

Images of the gargoyles of Notre Dame and Saint Merry

## Washington National Cathedral

## Chapelle Bethlehem, France

Everyone observes and investigates... No comment by me.

## Saint Merry Church

Gloomy place, heritage of humanity with strange and dark secrets.

The gargoyle that identifies Pazuzu, but Levi ignored him.

...He observed the different gargoyles that decorate the church, which inspired him.

His book is a basic treatise on occultism and magic themes. Where it mentions Baphomet, as the devil or evil, taking into account that Eliphas Levi for years devoted himself to the priesthood, he resigned on having observed the contradictions of the church. For not extend in the history of this incredible figure, I invite you to make a break in the reading and read his biography, it will be helpfully.

The image corresponds to the association of themes; gargoyles, philosophy, religion, have been the common symbol of modern Satanism, but it has also been an incredible propaganda for the assets of the church, which thanks to popularizing the image it has managed to get more parishioners and therefore profits.

All business is good, except the one that limits and condemns men and women, who in their beliefs are destroyed.

## Current Satanism

With the initial themes, it is understood that Satan is more than a devil, more than a biblical commentary; it is an entity, feared, a shadow that belongs to the underworld, not physical but mental, and an extreme knowledge that allows obtaining the power to dominate.

Among all, religion persecuted more vigorously the European philosophies of the world of the old religion, where it was cruel against Pagan ones, associating the great rituals of harvests, with the adoration of Satan, witches, magicians, sorcerers, healers, anyone who rebelled to the precepts was condemned and killed.

At Renaissance epoch, after the obscurantism, the Gothic world awakens, an epoch of different vision comes, the thinkers wake up and with them the world of the darkness and the darkness reborn, they slowly initiate the awakening of consciences.

The Church begins the fierce human carnage, in order to keep the creed, the truth, the hegemony of a monotheism and nothing better, that fight against the demon, is in this epoch where the church begins the demonization of everything that exists, but likewise, it is the awakening to the power of the secret.

# SATANISM

To enter the hell, is to enter the bottom of one of the most complex philosophies, the cradle of power, the force of acting, the total freedom of the spirit. The being born free and incorrupt, possesses a series of implicit knowledge, talents, different intelligences, capacity for psychic union with different aspects of the total wisdom of the cosmos.

Returning to the previous section of Pantheism where all knowledge, the absolute one, including demons and gods, is already vibrating in everything that exists, it is important to observe, if we have a moment of life, present, past and future, in that future that already exists itself, otherwise it would not have a new second, in that future everything is already done.

But, we live it, instant by instant, on the physical plane, but on the mental plane, time does not exist.

Well, calmly, this starts to get complicated.

If one thinks quickly which is the ritual of the pact with Satan to sell it the soul in exchange for wishes, and a thousand other things, he has to wait a little to get that, he will already understand it.

*Let's continue ...*

It is important to evaluate several topics, and try to understand some issues that seem unlikely, like for example this universe, where we live, it is not real, and however it is true.

A person that lives near death extracorporeal experience realizes that its essence does not interact with the physical world, which stops.

Let's look at something interesting, we talk about the same demon and it is better to go step by step.

# SOUL AND SPIRIT

Let's use the imagination; this will help you to obtain the best pact, but without having to sell the soul.

Let's say that the computer systems began in a basic way, in a chain of transformations and adaptations, never of evolution.

Let's look quickly at a process of entering and obtaining the information from a computer.

 A Minidisc

 Then it was followed by a cd.

 Later, a USB

And there, the history ends, now, today, everything is done, wirelessly.

In a second, a picture is taken in one place and by Internet everyone receives it.

These objects of data transmission and reception constitute an infinity wisdom, let's say hypothetically that, in the future, what will undoubtedly happen, virtual worlds will be created, although there are some, we are still out of them.

It cannot enter the matter into a virtual world, but the thought.

Let's play with the imagination, let's say we want to know what a merchant thinks, if the virtual world is created, instead of placing a usb or a cd, we place in a virtual being, with a "Soul" something similar to the avatar movie, which transmit information within the virtual world and also learn it.

But to make this work, we let you the total freedom of action, you will never know that you live in a virtual reality, you will have emotions, thoughts, dreams, desires and consciousness.

You are programmed so that after a time when its memory is full, you must leave the virtual world and bring the information with you.

It does not matter how you die, your apparent body is nothing more than renewable energy, in a renewable world that does not evolve.

Remember it is a virtual world, when this "being" die, the essence or memory is released which in the future will be energy, will, soul, spirit, which vanishes in the virtual world and enters to feed the "absolute" program of commerce, with all that it contains. A kind of Eywa.

On delivering that content, it is not empty, but one returns again to another virtual world, until to find the total wisdom.

A little further, for a moment think, how many beings, would be required for having the total wisdom and how many virtual words could be created.

And, whoever lives in those worlds will suppose that it is real, until he begins to create his own virtual universes within a virtual world. That, although it is real, it does not exist and as well as a fractal of knowledge up to infinity. Did you understand?

Is this world real?
If that being has total freedom, and understands the substantial unreality of his real world, he begins to feel that there is something else, that he can see the future, that he can alter his surroundings with his mind, he discovers that something inside him makes him different, he is free, totally free, when he understands it, he acts.

He takes by himself the power of creation and within his freedom, he creates.

But what would happen if we impose on these beings the religion and we tell them that they are creations of a distant god that they must find in the heavens, through the submission of their minds.

Remember the first program, he is a merchant, who is interested in obtaining a profit at whatever cost, and, what better than selling a god, perceiving that he dominates that reality. And those who get out of that business, easy, are eliminated.

If I told you that this world is similar to the virtual world, think for a moment, where is the evolution, what has really evolved? We see clones of the same, the crocodile that has 240 million years, it is still the same, the tiger, the lion, the spider, the world only has subtle changes, and if man would disappear from the earth, in a million years, there would be no trace of his existence.

What does changes?
Do we change pixels for atoms?
Usb, cd or wireless communication for soul?

Now a little further, if everything is energy, what happens when that being of the virtual world understands that he can affect all his surroundings, that can canalize through his thought the infinite energy of that virtual world creating without limit and affecting everything in his freedom, he would be a super-being, in other words, god, but ... How would make him for other beings of this virtual world understand it?

That is the main door of hell, now let's enter the infernal room, where the demon's room awaits us.

In the atrium of hell, there is an inscription, which prays.

**"Nothing exists, everything is real"**

**Mind and body, heaven and earth, above or below,
there is no difference, more than
for the eyes of those who see it.**

## FREEDOM

What is the freedom?

All the spirits, all the souls, which are incorporated into a body, are free, infinitely free, its etheric energy filled with knowledge, power and force it is impregnated in the later moment with the birth, it is born free.

Without limitations, without impositions, without sin, with all the power of Being, the seed of his spirit, only will develop in freedom.

But on having been born he is already being submitted, mentally castrated, programmed to decay, to kneel down, to be submissive of other minds, the tradition of the slavery is born and orders: Mutilate him!. You must circumcise him, it begins the holiday of happiness, the whole family gathers to look for the godfather, we must baptize him, and so Satan will get away from his soul.

The limitation of spirit, by the mind of others, who equal were born free but others limited them, and those to others for generations, all have committed the same crime, to sever power, to close the door of spiritual force.

Freedom is the right that all beings have to choose, to direct, to create and to build their future, without stereotypes, without dogmas, without creeds, without impositions, without religions, without Jurassic and useless traditions.

Freedom is the ability of the being to extract from his inner the power to face the life, to find responses, to discover the horizons.

When the limitation comes, they are imposed dogmas, he is condemned since he is born with the terrible history that he is already a sinner, who, without the baptism, will be culprit of the stupidity of others, he is condemned to obey blindly the laws of the god of the men.

He is indoctrinated, subjugated, submitted with infernal credence, of nastiness, without seeing the intensity of the evil that is committed, the total destruction of the spirit, there begins the calvary of his controlled, limited life, annulled like being, like person, and from then on up to the day of his death where in another absurd ritual they will try to save the soul. Which soul, save it from what? If his miserable existence of negation and limitation was a valuable life ruined, a wonderful opportunity destroyed.

All life is programmed, in negation, do not do, do not think, do not say, if you look do not touch, if you touch your hands should be amputated, if you wish you should annul the desire, you will not do anything different than the law does not refer you and order you.

Then the confirmation comes; the confirmation of submission, of brainwashing and the family celebrates, we must continue killing that spirit, that does not think, that does not fornicate, that does not want to fight, that does not prosper and if it does, is to enrich the church.

And this way ... you will receive the communion, the curse of life, you will eat and drink the poison of misery, every eight days you will have to confess, even to the most intimate of your life, what you did, what you thought, what you imagined, what you felt, what you tried to create, and all that, will be sin, you have no right to be or feel, but if your desire is strong, they will take advantage to satisfy the desire by saying, so you are consecrated to god, so that it is not sin, they rape, they rip the skin, they destroy the soul, is the secret of the consecration which nobody must know.

This way life begins, the woman slave, servile, impoverished, destroyed and submitted to the slavery, with the unhappy marriage, and the fatal judgment, "Until the death separates you". The whole life, the whole opportunity truncated in coarctation of freedom.

Freedom of Satanism is different, neither breaks the spirit nor fragments the soul, it is a support, encouragement, motivation, leadership; it is the freedom to discover the dynamic force of finding horizons and conquering them.

It is the power made flesh, feel and learn to feel, live and learn to live, fight for your ideals, do not submit yourself, don't have master or owner, or husband, or wife, you must be faithful only to one. "TO YOURSELF".

Make effort for be happy, enjoy the pleasures as you wish, everything that from your skin to your soul you want, and make you happy, do it without remorse.

Rape your rapist, always charge a little more of debt. Be fair in your life, but make respect it, since you are born you will respect your body and your life.

**The power of Satan, is:**
- Triumph not humiliation.
- Fight not slavery.
- Intelligence not force.
- Strategy not deception.
- Subtlety not aggression.
- The dominion over the weak.
- Life on the death.
- Love, to whom deserves it.
- Courage not sacrifices.
- Wealth not poverty.
- Strength not weakness.
- The preparation in the arts.
- The preparation in physical defense.
- The ability to merge with shadows
- To learn entering and altering dreams.
- To invoke the entities that keep secrets.

• To have the power to transform realities and everything you want, provided you understand that you are totally and infinitely total, free to do what you want to do! Everything, as far as your skin ends, you will respect deeply the freedom that hidden in another skin!

• You will not dominate anybody.

• You will not impose wishes use strategy.

• You will not have masters or executioners, fight for your life.

• Defend your life to where your force allows it.

• If you must destroy something that hurts you or threatens your existence, do it without repenting, it is your life.

• You will not use love as an excuse, love whoever deserves to be loved.

• You can have as many loves as you want, on condition that those loves want to have you.

• Liquidate your enemy, in any fight of life, if you leave him wounded he will liquidate you.

• Do not have friends, males or females; they will be your downfall.

• Do not believe, know.

• Live in the shadows and hide yourself in the light.

• Wear your cape and cover, be always unnoticed.

• Never in your life tell your secrets, if you do it... tomorrow they will be your condemnation.

• Be discreet.

• Do not presume.

• Do not boast.

• Concentrate and control your emotions or they will control you.

• Never in your existence make alliances, pacts or partnerships, you will end up betrayed.

• Dominate and command.

## Freedom of thought and decision

In the deep sense of the freedom of being, mental conditioning unfortunately occurs, before a being is born he is programmed to "live" according to what is imposed without right to free choice.

He is conditioned with precepts, rules, limits, it is imposed a tradition for tradition of the traditions, it is accepted without thinking or analyzing what is imposed, that being will never be Free!

In Satanism there is respect for that freedom, that free will that everyone possesses, from his skin inwards him.

It is depressing to see how one educates, since the beginning there are imposed the concepts of submission and surrender, threats, condemnations, punishments for thinking.

There is no freedom nor there is an opportunity to awaken consciousness in independent processes, no one baptizes himself, they baptize him.

Nobody discovers itself, they control him, since children are subjected to the choir, to mass, to suppose that life is a gift of a god of lies to which we have to thank everything, thanks god he approved the exam, thanks god he has a house, thanks god and god never did anything.

The demon nor did nothing except the paranormal phenomena of extraordinary force that obey with other kind of entities or powers, neither God nor the devil do nothing, because they simply ***do not exist!***. But, incredibly all the events are attributed to them, their presence is imposed, the one cannot exist without the other, fruit of the business of faith.

***Satanism is not a being; it is a philosophy of power latent in everyone, castrated in many by the dogmas of the faith.***

When inner power wakes up, the force of free spirit, when the imposed barriers are broken, it will be more than god and devil, the power of total freedom is obtained and in that freedom each one chooses to dominate life or be dominated, prey or hunter, success or failure.

## Freedom of Satanism

Every being on having been born, is entitled to choose without impositions.

## Freedom to be

A man cannot deny another man, which induces his deep pleasure, if this pleasure sublimates his soul.

Every being in his inner is free to choose what pleases him and dislikes him; each being in his inner possesses totally the right to live as he wishes.

How a man is allowed to judge whether another should eat this or that thing, whether or not he should enjoy his pleasures.

If he can or cannot do what gives him happiness and profit, how one can deny a skin the desire for another skin.

How is limited to who want to discover his limits, faster, higher, further; Can a man who didn't even try it, limit whom wishes it?

Tie the wings of a seagull since born, leave it this way for three years and then let it go, even if it has wings it will never be able to fly.

The only option in each being is to let him be free, to let him be, that in that freedom the spirit flows without limits, nor conditioning, allowing the inner wisdom to open like a flower in spring.

It is not to educate teaching ancient traditions; it is to educate canalizing implicit potentials, motivating, supporting, and demanding so that each being extracts more from him. It is regrettable to see that schools, kindergartens, education centers, universities, hospitals, courtrooms, and in each place, the first thing that can be seen is a damn bloody crucifix that recalls the total death of the spirit.

A crucifix represents the total death of freedom; it is the tie of the wings of the thought, the castrating figure of the spirit, the prison of the free will. And those who teach, there direct and order, they are only vassals of their own mental slavery, guardians of traditions of deep roots of mental misery.

It is taught about god and his enslaving laws, the fear to god is taught, the inability of man is taught, everything is god's work, one is guided in the path of the "Lord", it is taught to fall and never get up, to resign without to fight, to accept with devotion and gratitude the greatest of miserable lives.

It is taught to be a parasite of the universe, a being invaded by mental misery, it is taught to be something lower than miserable. And the worst, it is paid for learning that.

Religion class is taught in schools, in the universities literates boast talking about theology, they all speak of a god that does not exist, in the infinite lie of the prosperous business of limiting the soul and life.

Everything is a process of mental degradation, which is imprinted before birth.

Entire Nations, rulers, even in banknotes brainwashed with the phrase "In God we trust, may God protect you, that the Blessed Virgin protect you, etc."

Satanism advocates for freedom of beliefs, for respect with free expression and identity of each one with total denial to teach children the beliefs of traditions, and which Satanism tends to the free development of innate abilities in individuals, in the academic exchange, where areas of unusable knowledge negotiated with knowledge.

We have been teaching for many years what does not work, educating towards impoverishment, but we do not teach to wake up, we do not increase the inner knowledge that exists in each one, the great painter who starts painting the wall of the house, must be punished, the great merchant who sells sweets in the classroom, must be expelled, the great thinker and philosopher must be confined in an mental hospital.

It is not difficult for those who read these lines, to see reflected in them segments of their own existence.

The restricted freedom is a freedom wasted in a lifetime, the worst of the cells without guards, or shackles, the prison of the thought.

At the same moment of an ejaculation, an ovule prepares himself, two million spermatozoids are expelled, each with an incredible load of wisdom and knowledge, two million that compete in the most incredible olympiad of obstacles, all use innate strategies, all they fight, they all display a thousand percent of their power, to triumph.

And only one wins, one of two million or one billion, one, the best, the strongest in the inner strength that is, yes, the engine that impels it.

They all are equal, physically and genetically, everyone should win, but something extraordinary impregnated in the deepest of their core moves them, the one that most release that power will triumph. Congratulations!

You are a winner over more than two million, a warrior of life. If you read these lines and understand them, it is because you have won.

Now, the power is still latent inside you in the depths of your being, but very few continue liberating that force, have been mentally annulled, destroyed, finished, the wings of thought severed, and thrown into the unhappiness and misery of god.

And the worst thing about a life wasted is to follow a race of businessmen who have profits by selling a god of lies.

The only way that a being makes his power free, it is allowing himself to be free! And that freedom is what determines if it fights or is defeated.

As when it was a sperm, now he must face the life, must overcome the barriers, the obstacles, must be demanded, among more initial difficulties present to him stronger he will be.

The only way is to allow keeping alive the wild freedom.

Have you seen how a dog is trained since birth?

Although, it is very easy, in many families dogs that do not know about religions, dominate their masters.

It is easy to see the dog pulling and dragging to the master, few dogs are behind.

The dog does not know languages or idioms; it is trained only with power and harmony. Human error is that they train them with words. Get up, sit down, kneel down, come, go, and just like any dog that obeys, give it the cookie as prize, go and sit down, and then pay for be trained.

A good Satanist technique to release power is to learn to train a dog, without speaking a single word, only with a thought, looks and energy. Try it and you will discover how the world is trained.

A total freedom is based on healthy rebelliousness.

• Not with concepts imposed.
• Not with the servile obedience of other interests.
• Not with parental influence like imposition.
• Not with the acceptance of complacencies to others.
• Not with subjection.
• Not with servility.

- Not with imposition of beliefs.
- Not with the humiliation of love.
- Not with begging.

Every being works and builds his destiny without the influence of others, parents who want their children to be, spouses who nullify, boyfriends or girlfriends who control, employers who oppress.

The church, guilty of all human misfortunes, imposes without reason degrading precepts of the human being, always inducing obedience, sacrifice, resignation, submission to the will of a fictitious god and therefore spiritual delivery of devotion to the church, even the name with which he is identified must be imposed int the worst sign of death: the baptism.

## Sexual freedom

In Satanism there is an important premise, there is no sexual gender, all beings are androgynous, half woman, half man.

There is no commitment or marriage, everyone is free to give and receive love by anyone, and everyone is free to leave whenever he wants.

The responsibility of a life is the total value of life, if one is assumed, one should respond with one's own.

In Satanism it is not sex that dominates reason, it is reason that dominates sex, therefore, pollution and abuse is avoided, the body is the sacred temple of the spirit, not depraved orgies, pedophilia, the sex abuse, Satanism is not the corruption of the body and the mind in pursuit of unnecessary pleasures, it is the enjoyment of free pleasure.

Sexuality is to enrich the spirit with the freedom of feeling, nobody can be guardian and caretaker of the genitals and desires of anyone, without ties or mental locks, and sexual freedom is the responsibility of everyone.

It is important in this theme the respect of legal cohabitation laws, as well as cultural laws of each region, is not by and based in freedom the right to damage, torture, destroy, impose, submit, constrain to another looking for pleasure.

It is important to recognize that sexuality is an agreement, consent among those who want it, not a business or a violation of desire.

Sexuality is the mutual experience of a consensual pleasure, freedom of giving and receiving, without precepts of limitation or laws that protect it.

A woman and a man can have as many partners as they want, none will be the property of another; respect, support, friendship, attention, free love, are the bastions of sexual freedom.

Sexual tendencies are inherent to individuals, free from social and legal condemnations, free from the thoughts of any being that in his pride imposes his thinking on the freedom of another.

Gender equality between men and women is equity, the wrong concept of a male god, completely nullified the value of women, it is still the time where the stupid fable of creation is considered real, if god made the woman from the rib of Adam, genetically only another Adam could be born.

But the sexist dogma of god, created with a history of lies, the submission of women to men and to the own god.

The differences between woman and man are physical, not mental and much less spiritual, just an outside penis in the man, and an inner penis with womb or uterus, that's all.

The breasts ... men have the same breasts than women and they produce breast milk, it's called gynecomastia.

Every sexual act implies responsibility for one's life and that of others, despite the individual freedom, not you

It must not break the freedom of others; never in Satanism there will be the imposition.

## Freedom to love

Every being is free to express his love in the way his soul projects it, any time it does not exceed the tenderness or hurt what is loved.

Love is not a business where one expects to receive what was given or more than what was given, love is free without ties or contracts, it is born from freedom and it is delivered freely without miserly or visceral interests, love does not possess nothing, for not to be possessed by anything.

Love is the dynamic force that motivates the spirit, strengthening the will, it is the ability to feel and merge two or more bodies, in a single soul.

There are no owners of love, no one can belong to anyone, and nobody delivers a love that asks or demands, love gives itself to whoever is the fruit of love.

"It has been said love your enemies, love those who hurts you, love and you will be loved".

Matthew 5 44-48Reina-Valera 1960 (RVR1960)

44 But I say you: love your enemies, bless them who curse you, do good to those that hate you, and pray for them which despitefully use you and persecute you.

A clear sample of mental conditioning, in Satanism does not exist such a thing, love the one who deserves it and for enemies there is only the condemnation. If it is done well to who does wrong, when he will stop doing wrong, if every time he does it he is rewarded? For those that outrage only remains an outrage two times more strong.

Love is not a defeat, it does not recognize failures, love is the highest emotion produced by the most intense devotion of love or the most intense of hatreds.

Hate is the love injured, deceived, bought, subdued, submitted, hate is the vibration of a tainted love, hate is forgetfulness and the condemnation of revenge, and the best revenge is contempt for what once was loved.

Love, is not the sacrifice so that others live, it doesn't clean sins, it does not redeem the murderer in forgiveness, love is not a crucifix of lies that announces the delivery of life by love of lies, professed to win love in the treacherous business of faith.

Love is free ... in the highest expression of freedom; hate is free in the highest expression of freedom.

## Dignity

"If they slap you, put the other cheek, that is said, if they ask for your cape, give also the shirt, love whoever hurts you".

Dignity is the respect that is professed, likewise, and the respect that is professed whoever is worthy of respect.

The kind and compassionate person is an unworthy useless that does not consider the damage caused in his goodness.

The one who forgives is the most unworthy; the one who understands is the worthy one who deserves all respect. The man who kneels down before another man, the woman who kneels down before his executioner are the most unworthy pusillanimous beings who do not respect themselves nor deserve respect.

The one who begs and cries, the one who asks, the one who cries, the one who suffers from self-pity, the one who asks on his knees for mercy, are cowards that do not deserve even the pity they demand.

The worth one has honor, strength, tenacity, the respect is not imposed, is won with sturdy demonstrations of effort, fight and conquer.

To be worthy is to have the ability to harden feelings; to have the strength and character not to succumb without fighting; to be worthy is to overcome adversity without falling into impoverished sentimentality.

What does dignity exist in whom without fighting accepts humbly his destruction and that of others? The being, he is debated in the handle of feelings, the scam of the fear that annuls the dignity with the promise and hope of a change, the unworthy ones as the righteous ones will first arrive in the sky of the abhorrence of existence.

He is not worth:
• Who kneels
• Who claims mercy
• Who prays and begs God
• Who accepts to be humiliated
• Who gives up without a fight
• Who waits without reason
• Who accepts forgiveness
• Who forgives
• Who is not respected
• Who is not appreciated
• Who is missing to his principles
• Who lies

The courage of the spirit, the strength of the will, the righteousness, the serenity of the action, is characteristic of being worthy.

## Freedom: good and evil

There are no good or evil, although the common thought accepts their existence as two antagonistic events with reference to a same event of freedom, win or lose.

Two words that have created countless theories, based on religions and struggles, two concepts tied with freedoms, concepts are imposed by fanaticism overwhelmed in unworthy beings that profess them.

An individual consideration that later becomes of group and is imposed like a concept.

Ideologies suggest a philosophy they assume like good, which should be imposed as the best option, considering the other or others like bad.

It is the game without end of two concepts moved by an interest, the only interest that is worth: the power.

Good and evil two extremes of freedom, a reflection of themselves in different optics. Good for one, undoubtedly evil for another. Evil for one, undoubtedly good for another. All the enemies are bad for each side.

To this must be added that a miserable god, with human attributions, god of misfortune and misery is considered good, and obviously for who does not agree with that postulate, is bad.

Since majority wins it is good, the minority will always be bad. Even the scales changes in the power game.

In Satanism there is no good or evil, there is no power than that lies in the interior of every being.

In Satanism there is **The Strategy!** Which has allowed that, although it is the element to fight the one that produces more wealth to the church, is still alive and now with more forces, it could never be silenced.

Satanism is strategy to obtain the greatest possible profit with the least effort, this way while they get worn in fighting it, they have strengthened it.

Have you ever seen a lioness lurking? Looking to? Into the brain of a lioness, obviously it does not think like the human beings, but it does something incredibly precise, its brain codifies a countless codes that give it an information, the corporal language of the prey, big, small, healthy, sick, if it has weapons, if it can hurt it.

It calculates the distance and the possible options about the route that the prey will take, it observes everything, the wind to prevent from taking its smell and betray it, that there are no hyenas, everything like a whole is codified, while doing this, internally it floods its body with adrenaline, its muscles are prepared, the claws contract like triggers ready to shoot.

Finally, in that analysis it makes an assessment, how much energy it must spend to catch the prey and how much energy it will produce to it. It chooses carefully the one that brings the most profit with the minor expense.

With that information done in a millisecond, it acts. It uses the best strategy and gets its profit.

Well for the lioness, bad for the prey, but the prey has advantages too, that's why there are more preys than lions.

Everything in nature acts under the same principle the strategy, even the concept of god is a strategy of business and enrichment, without selling anything, just words written in a book that produce millions and millions, out of the incredible political associations, companies created to dominate and to exploit, centers where they do not educate but they brutalize castrating the thought.

The lioness makes the total expense and the lion enjoys without fighting. It is the best strategist.

The religion that speaks so much about evil, has used the best strategy, much gain and power with minor effort, the selling of faith is since and for all life. How much money does a family pay throughout its life, in a constant bleeding dry, and what really does it receive back? What is the profit? Nothing, just a thought of gratitude to god for the work with which he pays the priests.

Good or evil, it depends on the optics; strategy is the technique of triumph and wins without competing or fighting.

The current world in all the social levels debates in the same sense, the scale goes from micro to macro, like the lion, we have the same concept, rarely applied, except when the need urges, that need that since one is born it was necessary to promote in every being, we have the same code to evaluate cost-benefit, is part of the philosophy of the Satanism, learn to be the hunter and not the prey.

The strategy is used when learning the art, who makes it comes directly out of the common dominator, surely a person without employment and with needs, discovers the way to make money selling a product or executing a job, he uses the strategy to improve, it will never be used again.

And, if he goes further, he will hire employees, his business will grow.

Everyone has implicitly the power of strategy; only few manage to break the wall imposed by religion freeing their minds from the yokes of the dogma.

With this premise, good and evil, it is a concept that everyone, according to his vision, considers.

In reality there is nothing good or evil, only strategy.

## The sin

Religion found the path of dominion through sowing the guilt complex in others, considering aberrant, denigrating, evil, sinful, impure, dishonest, treacherous and shameful any act, including a thought.

But ... with the greatest hypocrisy that may exist in the world, the lackey priests of god, condemn in others the deepest and most profane aberrations they do behind the doors of the church.

A god that impels disdain and greed, the most obscure and unprintable way of sodomy and pedophilia, the church's stigma.

For them, god consecration; for the faithful the deepest sins.

A virtuous woman, mother, without husband is called a "single mother" and she must be expelled from the community.

A woman not found virgin, on having married, must be repudiated, condemned and killed by stoning.

A man that rebels to god must be burned at the stake. Whoever feels sexual desires, must cut the hands used to masturbate.

A woman who feels sexual desires must mutilate herself.

A woman that is menstruating will be impure, unclean and must stay away.

All this and much more for god, is sin.

## A conflict among nature, reason and god

The nature provided man and woman with sensations, desires, bodies, strength, intelligence, beauty, an intense pleasure in procreation, an incredible force in women during ovulation, a power without limits in men of fortitude and decision.

The reason shows that there is no sin, there is no submission, reason comes into conflict when other reasons refuse the reason, the reason includes the incredible contempt and contradiction of god.

If you look at and feel, rips the eyes.
Look, but not touch.
If you want touch, get married.
Don't desire, hurt you to control your desire.
If you get excited, confess yourself, maybe the priest calms you down.
If you want money, get it, but donate it to your church.

If you're beautiful woman or man, it's vanity of vanities, burn your face or cut your nose, this way you will take away the desire from you.

If your noble parts act instinctively, burn them. This way you'll keep away of you the evil.

Everything is sin, the confession miserable element of condemnation, effective weapon to subdue.

Aberrant, it may be thought, but it is the cruel reality, millions of people today unmask the lowest and basest passions of the church, which, hidden behind an investiture of divine power, have disgraced the life of millions.

Every eight days, you must tell your secrets, every eight days you are being trained, every eight days, you must kneel down before another man with thoughts and acts thousand times worst that yours and he will give you forgiveness, you are now ready to receive communion in the mass, like a servile and trained dog, you will receive the cookie that will erase your sins.

Your communion with god is nothing more than perversion and manipulation, that god if he existed, would be the greatest and most corrupt sinner.

## Marriage

The greatest human stupidity, the death of love, the total slavery of the woman who must be submitted, but the church has all the manipulation weapons, the premarital course; two stupid old and bitter nuns, full of repressed desires, educate women as lovers, as slaves, as women should accept slavery as servants of the lord.

Annulling the greatness of each woman, the power that nature granted as life-giving.

What does a priest or a nun know about marriage? How do they know how many sexual poses the Kama Sutra has, the best antidote to keep love alive?

How do they know what is the responsibility of a close relationship, miserably condemned to misfortune, with the worst curse that can exist "Until death separates you"?

Out of this, the promise of eternal life; another sophism, heaven and hell, condemnation or salvation, and every year, they send the reminder for the sung mass of the dead people anniversary. And this without speaks about the celebrations of holidays until the day when the Virgin Mary had sex.

# The bible and Satan

A giant business with good performance cannot exist without a good product. The god's selling to assure its success undoubtedly needs an element of sale: Satan or the devil. Curiously, the bible names in an unfinished way 52 times to Satan and 33 times the demon.

Throughout the text references to Satan are cross-references with other texts, where the devil is alluded to, but ... no text really defines the concept. More than the Adversary, approximate meaning of the word Satan.

The rest have been elements added over the years, obtaining in Satan the enemy that must be destroyed, base of the church, is the fight between god and the devil.

It is important to clarify that before the arrival of the Jewish ones to Egypt or the Israel people, the polytheism or conception of many gods existed, then monotheism is created, with a single god, which produces that the other existing gods become demons.

The church based on the bible, is the only religion in the world, with different names, which has imposed its creed through massacres, robberies, rapes, destruction, politics, inquisition, crusades, leading the world to the worst misfortune of the war.

## What is the Bible?

A little history, near the River Nile the Papyrus plant is born with which leaves and books known as bibles are made. The Bible is a book made of papyrus. Up to there, nothing sacred.

### From where the history is born

The Sumerian people existed 6,500 years BC, a highly cultured people with a series of histories and legends, both the creation of the world and the Sumerian religion.

In this era where writing begins in Baghdad, cradle of the current culture, the "Epic of Gilgamesh" was transcribed and the origin of the Sumerian religion was twisted, a total copy, that is the Bible, the grossest deception to humanity and the most blatant cultural theft.

The sum of all these songs and ancient poems are the original source of the Bible including and plagiarizing histories and legends of other peoples such as the birth of Moses, original text of the Mahabharata.

"When Kunti was a pubescent girl, her stepfather put her in the service of the fussy saint Durvasas, who was visiting. Durvasas, pleased with the lack of self-esteem of the young Kunti, gave him the blessing of invoking any god to have divine descendants. Just Durvasas left the Palace, the innocent Kunti, full of curiosity, invoked the god of the Sun, Surya. When this mentioned her that blessing included necessarily sexual intercourse, Kunti refused, because by losing her virginity she could no longer marry (according to the rigid Hindu caste society cannons). Surya replied that after sex he would rebuild the hymen so that her husband could not deduce that she was not virgin.

Kunti became pregnant, and according to the Mahabharata she gave birth instantly to her child. As the descendant of a god, he was born with ear lobes pierced by large gold rings, so Kunti called him Karna (ears). As she could not have this child, she put him in a clay pot and left him in the River Ganges. She prayed to Ganga (the goddess ruler of the river) to protect him. The child was educated by shudras, and ended up being known as Radheya."

The first part of the Bible are narratives that until the year 370 of our era, at the third Council of Carthage towards the year 397 was merged with the previous edition of the old testament. In other words 370 years after the supposed existence of Jesus, the whole history is created, with a deeper look was the element that allowed the invasions in the Mediterranean and the struggles that even today continue in the Middle East.

God neither exists nor inspires any prophet, and much less is the writer of the bible. The bible prevailed throughout the world as the sacred book, not accepted like a philosophy of life, but to avoid being vilely murdered.

In all this history, other beings with great knowledge were called Satan, demons and adversaries ... the bearers of freedom of thought. After this little compendium of the philosophy of Satanism, let's enter the magical world of power of this incredible philosophy.

# SATANISM

Satanism out a great philosophy gathers in its context a series of powers of incalculable force, to release them it is required the full understanding of the power that is latent but lies asleep inside the thought.

It is the beginning of the sacred pact between knowledge and its action in life.

**To the reader**
Let be this the time to clarify the reader:

• The supposed power of god increases with the concept that *"You will have everything without doing anything"* or in other words, god will grant you the miracle of healing, to get a husband with money, to pay your debts, to heal yourself, to get job, beauty, money, fortune, etc., all the caprices and desires, god grants them in change you pay and go to mass and; etc. and do nothing different to pray.

• The supposed concept of a pact with the devil is the same thing, wait for *"You will have everything without doing anything"* or in other words that the pact will give you everything you want and I regret to say you, it is not so.

But don't get discouraged so quickly, there is no divine or evil being in the universe that works to please you, but ... there is a power that is inside you that will give you what you want and more, but... you have to act. So, if it leave mental laziness, put into practice and include the following topics, you will get the power without having to ask.

**"It is my responsibility to clarify that when you start this type of knowledge your mind will vibrate on another scale of consciousness, where supernatural**

**and paranormal events will begin to occur in your life." Are you sure to continue, is it your freedom?**

The following themes ... will open the doors of the underworld, the phenomena and random events are the cause of the legends of demon power associated with Satan, the worst real enemy of all this is your own fear, you are the one who controls every event, you are the owner of the power. You decide...

To possess and to liberate a power is a big responsibility, the Satanism more than be a philosophy is the door to another universe, it is not a game, it is the understanding to use wisely the energy in one's own benefit, that knowledge obscured by religions, is there, where you are.

*"When opening a door one cannot stop what comes through it"*

# BAPHOMET AND SATANISM SYMBOLOGY AND PHILOSOPHY

Thousands of meanings have been given to this symbol, and this will be one more, the first five-pointed star, pentagram and other names with which it is known, was discovered in the population of Ur, with a 3,500 years old, but it can be older for many thousands of years. There is no way to estimate time in a non-organic object.

Now well, for what did the Sumerians create a five-pointed star enclosed in a circle? Ockham's razor says "The simplest and sufficient explanation is the most probable, but not necessarily the true one"

Let's use a little logic, suddenly this symbol is attractive, but it has nothing to do with Satanism, if it has not been integrated by its form or representation, and before this all interpretations are valid, there is no absolute truth about this.

## Sumerian Tablet

It is probable only probably that due to the location of Ur, the Sumerians designed a kind of weather-vane to measure the winds or the beginning and end of the seasons, but the attractive of the symbol and its ease implementation has given for many symbolic interpretations.

Among them the one of greater acceptance corresponds with the pagan world or world of the witches the old religion, which was adopted to represent simultaneously

four elements: Fire, Earth, Air and Water, and the power of the spirit, together with the cycle of the Sabbath or seasons. An exact relationship with the Chinese culture and its five elements. For this reason as regards Baphomet, it would represent the domain over nature, natural intelligence, cosmic secrets, etc.

The knowledge of the different spheres in which nature vibrates, allows the influences, the effects, the realization of alterations both in the mental sphere and in the physical field, this knowledge about the psychic alterations produced by the lunar influence and the seasons, alter the environment, sowing, cultivation and harvest, life, death, attraction and repulsion, changes and mutations, all content in the five pointed star. To know these subtle variations give the power for who dedicate themselves to the magical arts.

However, throughout the ages this symbol became an icon, which just by observing it triggers a state of consciousness that induces mystery, power, the strange and supernatural, polypsychism, many minds united in a common thought they end up giving a halo of life to this figure.

## The body of Baphomet

BAPHOMET
KNIGHTS TEMPLARS' GOD

# ANDROGYNOUS

Let us enter into a very complex theme that requires a certain mental freedom, observing the body of Baphomet, implicitly has a series of representations of great wisdom.

To start it is the living representation of roman God Faunus, or Greek God Pan. Owner of forests, harvests, crops, droves, it belongs to the magical world of fairy world, its existence is presumed to be real, in recent years there are some graphic documents that show it. The Faun or God Pan are the basis of the concept that everything is energy or god and that god or energy is in everything, and everything in that energy.

From God Pan is born the old religion of Pantheism that considers that everything is god, not a single being, but all beings and all things, a philosophy obviously condemned by the church that has humanized this energy, converting it into a god whom it is necessary to adore and to pay him.

Pan and the Faunus represent a male goat, half man half goat, always accompanied by nymphs and satyrs, magical beings of nature, and the church skillfully converted elementals into angels.

In this aside appears a syncretism among these gods, with pagan rituals, during the Sabbath of Samhain, at the end of the agricultural year men who dedicated to

hunting, used as a costume the flagstaffs or head of a male goat, which at the same time represents the god Cernunnos.

These gods represent nature, with all its mysteries, the power of the old religion, the wisdom to achieve portents, the strength of the verb power in spells, enchantments, divination, sorcery, witchcraft, all these and more elements of the magical religion, they served for the church to create the devil, those who practiced that pagan knowledge should die at the stake ... just as information ...

Paganism is not a religion; a pagan is a peasant or man from the field, as well as heretic that means opponent or adversary very similar to the meaning of Satan.

Apart the gods Faunus and Pan, the body of Baphomet represent the androgynous, the anatomical reality that all people are at the same time, a duality of gender, male and female.

A complex theme and very old so much so that the same Plato already talk about it, to understand a little more, we must observe the human anatomy, in which you will find as only difference an internal genital organ and one external, otherwise the body is identical.

This equality awakens the senses and without doubt criticism, today there are known the different hormonal alterations that produce physical and mental changes regardless the body that you have.

Gynecomastia, or enlarged breasts in men, accompanied by increased prolactin or breast milk, shows that anatomically doesn't exist a real greater difference, fat or muscle, external and internal organs.

The androgynous is the representation of equality, fertility, the free sexuality, spiritual development, the creative force of nature that does not define genders or stereotypes.

Baphomet represents a whole in balance, light and darkness, female and male, child and adult, life and death, constant mutation of life, the wheel of the cycles in the development of power.

Not the denial that the church imposes and condemns. It is the vehicle of life, the transit among life, death, the advancement and retreat, gain and loss, the philosophical and sexual androgynous.

The attraction is not produced from man to woman, but from the femininity of one with the masculinity of other.

In the ancient tantric philosophy of sacred sexuality, the art of sexual transmutation of kundalini serpent that ascends and descends according to sexual impulse.

Is to remember that in Satanism like in Tantra, sexual gender does not exist, the integration of two energies through the skin, without constraints or contracts, itself, Satanism tends to bisexuality and pansexuality, in total freedom of the individuals to profess it freely.

The concept of creation is contrary to human nature, woman is minimized since the beginning of genesis to the state of subordination, machismo appears to such an extent that the priests, condemned women as sinful, turned sexuality into the most sinful and forbidden, repudiated and condemned act.

But the church in its double morality even the same bible in many of its sections makes direct allusion. Sexuality of the bible.

"Deuteronomy 23:1-2Reina-Valera 1960 (RVR1960)

23 It'll not enter into the Congregation of the Jehovah who has injured testicles, or amputated his virile member."

Deuteronomy 24Reina-Valera 1960 (RVR1960)

24 When some will take woman and will marry her, if he'll not like her for having found in her any indecent thing, he'll write her divorce letter and he'll give it into her hand, and he'll get out her from his house.

Leviticus 21

17. Speak to Aaron and tell him: none of your descendants throughout their generations, having some defect, will approach to offer the bread of their God.

18 Because no male in whom would be defect will approach him; man blind or cripple, or mutilated, or bold,

19. or male who has broken foot or broken hand,

20. or hunchback, or dwarf, or having the cloud in the eye, or that has scabies, or instep, or bruise testicle

1 Samuel 18

1 And when he had finished speaking with Saul, the soul of Jonathan was linked with David's, and Jonathan loved him as to his own soul.

2 And Saul took him that day, and did not let him go back to his father's house.

3. And Jonathan and David made a covenant because him loved him as his own soul.

And Jonathan undressed clothing that had on him

2 Samuel 1

26 Anguish I have for you, my brother Jonathan, that you were me very sweet for me: most wonderful was your love than the love of the women"

There are too many themes to transcribe, but you find them in the book *"Viaje al Apocalipsis" [Journey to the Apocalypse]*.

What is not understood when reading the texts, if god has the power to heal, why did not he heal the testicles or the member of his future priests? Simple, god does not exist, and neither the devil.

The pleasure of the flesh is the fertility of the soul; the sexual freedom in all its infinite limit of possibilities is the representation of the Baphomet's body

In Satanism, sexuality is a living demonstration of life, far from feelings, far from dogmas, far from impositions of commitments and contracts, it is the absolute freedom of being shared, generating this way the most sublime free love.

But ... the church was in charge of turning sex into a couple's business, a prostitution disguised as miserly interests, the total subjection of women by the total imposition of man.

It turned the believers into the most wretched and unhappy ones by imposing a marriage to justify sexuality, it established as a requirement the virginity of the woman by turning everybody into the genital custodians of them.

Today, in that brainwashing of limitations, we see with sadness the annulment of women in all the expression of the word. Woman!, the condemnation, the repudiation, the vexation, the feminicide, the systematic destruction of her possibilities like human.

Satanism, on the contrary, dignifies the woman, exalts her in the pregnant power of giving birth to life.

The church has been the promoter of the destruction of the true feeling of loving in freedom. But, behind the walls of the temples and seminaries, hide the most unprintable sexual aberrations that anyone can imagine, the double morality of the church.

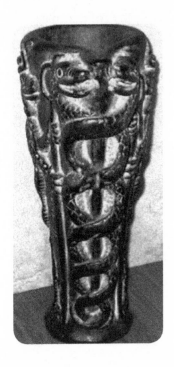

The oldest caduceus that exists, representation of the god Ningishzida, belonging to the Sumerian people, more than 10,000 BC.

# CADUCEUS OF HERMES

In the middle of Baphomet, highlights the caduceus of God Hermes, or the God Thot, or the God Mercury. Really they are the same, but from different cultures, Greek, Egyptian and Roman. Three representations of the same content, three wise people with extraordinary knowledge in the transmutation of thought and hermetic secrets that change time and destiny.

## Thoth

**Thot or Dyehty,** Egyptian god of wisdom, for being the administrator of the mental powers was known as the "Bull of the stars" Thoth

leaves his teachings for humanity in the different tablets known as the Egyptian tarot. (See the book of Thoth)

## Hermes and Mercury

Both the God Hermes the scribe of the gods as the God Mercury of the romans, share the same characteristics, really they are the same, Mercury represents the mind and the intellect, the astuteness and the strategy, vision and action, Hermes represents the wisdom, the mutation, the creative force.

 In the middle of Baphomet, appears the Caduceus of Hermes, the masterpiece of the wisdom and hermetic philosophy, a compendium of teachings, strange, but with great power in applying them.

This is the main base of the great work and the mental power for those who know how to apply it and discover its deep content.

It is of great importance to clarify that the church syncretized the original texts of Hermetic philosophy in the supposed existence of Hermes Trimegistus, trying to subtract the power of ancient alchemy *(see the book La Magia de la Alquimia [The Magic of Alchemy]).*

Hermes, is the same Hermes Trimegistus, this affirmation is found in the different tarot sheets, but ... again the church, during the Vth century when the Egyptian original papyrus were translated, St. Augustine of Hippo, a great scholar of different cultures with a knowledgeable knowledge follower of Manichaeism, resigns to surrender to Christianity, it is in this part where he transforms the discourses of Hermes, adducing him like a prophet of god, fortunately, the original texts and nearby translations belie the church in its eagerness to christianize the hermetic contender.

**Hermes** transmits a great and extensive knowledge, difficult theme to deal with in all its content in this grimoire.

For which I refer only to the topic that concerns us about Baphomet and the caduceus of Hermes.

## THE CADUCEUS

The Caduceus of Hermes is taken as a basis, but concerning the Caduceus of the oldest Sumerian creator God Ningishzida, there is no information about its use and meaning, just the mute object.

The Caduceus of Hermes a strange gift of Apollo, in exchange, Hermes presents the magic flute or panpipe to Pan, but as everything has been transformed according to the whims of the artists, the Caduceus of Hermes may have been very different.

Probably the caduceus would be something similar with the rod of power of the God Ptah, an Anj, crowned with the Dyed.

However, the real information has been lost throughout history.

Now, the caduceus represents the acting principles of mental alchemy to work miracles or supernatural alterations, the dominion of the mind over the universe.

Three important sections in the development of paranormal phenomena appear with the representation of the caduceus that in it represents the hermetic philosophy. Theme that will be treated later the basis of mental power and transformation.

# DOORS TO THE UNDERWORLD

Let's start, the underworld is the deepest part of your mind, it's a state of the soul that breaks reality, therefore, beings of other dimensions, normally known as demons, so you will feel, you will see and they will appear beings from other dimensions, usually known as demons, but it is just a name, more simple, entities of the beyond.

To unleash the power we must first understand something very interesting, you are, you has been and will be, time does not exist, everything is self-contained in an eternal present.

Now well, a little attention with the following theme, knowledge or wisdom existed, exists and will exist in the same present, let's think about the current world making a comparison, if you want to know or have the idea of something, use your browser and write a question, somewhere in the world someone wrote something related to what you want to know and you get the information.

Something similar happens in the spiritual world, but there is no another different navigator than your thought, by existing in this plane, the spiritual plane has been left aside, where all the wisdom exists, let us say like example that in the universe millions of bubbles float, each of them with determined information, when you want to know something you get connect with this information. Remember the apart of Tesla's inspiration.

# THE POWER OF SATAN

This is perhaps one of the parts of this grimoire more desired and expected, the power, how to obtain it, how to develop it, how to control it.

Before entering this door of the hell, it is prudent to remember something, if you have reached this point without reading the rest of the book, I ask you with all respect, I ask you, please do not follow.

You are going to open a door, moved by a desire and wish to obtain secrets and wisdom, of great strength, of great energy, but terrible and macabrely dangerous, when invoking the power, the superior force, without knowing how to be in balance and to control it, which will undoubtedly lead your life to darkness, and you, and, only you will be responsible for your actions.

An anxious being, eager to find shortcuts to achieve your goals without fighting, you will not have mental capacity to handle a power of immeasurable strength and energy. You will end being victim of the thoughts that you can not avoid, you will open a door, without being prepared, you will end with a fight inside... without being able to control it, this section is not a read-only, it is a secret revealed, if you understand it, assimilate it, step by step, you will awaken a state of consciousness without equal.

When crossing the threshold of this door, one enters the deepest of the darkness, where the perpetual darkness is, where the knowledge and wisdom are hidden, only for spirits that can be seen without seeing.

It is important to note several points.
• The entire existing universe is an illusion.
• All events of destiny may be altered.
• All future exists here and now.
• All your wishes can be realized.
• Everything that exists does not exist.
• Everything is and is not.
•All is nothing and nevertheless it is EVERYTHING.
• Your mind is the light that uncovers the veil of the night.
• The hidden power should not be revealed to anyone, it is a secret in your soul.
• You must have courage before the unknown.

Everything is real and unreal; this must be understood in the deepest part of your being.

## Influences on the physical plane

After open this door, slowly, change, knowledge and wisdom will emerge in your life, through different channels, a radio program, a television program, a song, an event, a trivial event, a phrase heard unexpectedly, a stranger who talks to you.

Your mind will initiate a change, you will see the life and the flow of the days differently, you will feel in your inner an awakening, sensations never perceived, changes in your appearance, deep desires of discipline, the imperative need to exercise your body, and everything will come to your life in the way you least imagine, so you should be aware of the signs.

## Mental influences

I just transcribe what is written on the stone, where the flames discover the strange words that do not have human translation, but only it is possible to transcribe the sensations that they produce.

Once again I must warn you, it is still time to renounce this treatise, only if you consider that you have understood the above, only if you consider that you have the ability to control your mind and your thoughts, polarizing and quieting your spirit, that your intention is controlled by reason, continue; otherwise, strengthen your mind first, daily exercise your body strongly, this will help you to maintain control and strengthen your will.

If you consider that you are not prepared, keep this book locked up in a black mantle, until you are sure about the decision you should make, as a suggestion, read again all the section, until you return to this point, then you will know what to do.

By mentally accepting the knowledge of power, the door to the world of shadows will open, when your mind is in a trance state, during sleep, when your consciousness is absent, your inner self, your spirit will vibrate in a different scale, where you will have contact with the world of darkness and wisdom.

It must be clear that after a time, a series of visions will begin, not only in dreams, but also during the vigil, you will perceive shadows that hide, breezes covering you, aromas, you will perceive a change in the environment and you will feel presences.

You may ask, are they demons? The answer is No, it is you, on another and other scales of different consciousness from what till now you have known joined to different entities.

For a moment you must meditate and think, if the spirit that is inside your body is eternal and indestructible, that is not subjected to time and space, for a moment think, to how many spaces and times of space and time you can reach.

Until now your spirit and your knowledge have been limited by your mind, by your knowledge, by the negation, of ¡I cannot! Your mind is your worst barrier.

# Training the mind

Please undress you, yes, as you read it, to the temple of wisdom one enter naked, you must do the following, about midnight, when the moon is in its waning phase, you should lie on your bed, naked and laid down, on the contrary to how you normally sleep, your head to your feet, and your feet to your head.

I ask you please, read first the text and then realize the whole exercise. Here where you are in this moment and if possible to do it, one of your hands, put the fingertips extended, without existing any kind of tension.

Please focus your atención on your fingertips, until you could perceive throbbing of your heart, take necessary time until you get it.

Feel in your fingers your own throb, focus, and enter ... with your mind ... in your body ...

Try to concentrate the sensation exclusively on different fingers, go from one to another, all or only one, now ... feel the little fingers ... in the thumbs ... in the thumbs finger ... practice until you get it ...

When you have perceived this first section, try to do it with your hands separated, when you consider that you have achieved it, prepare yourself for the midnight experience.

For this experience, it is required not to have dinner, lie down naked, without a pillow, straight... you will close your eyes and start a journey to your inner, you must concentrate deeply without care anything more.

You will feel the rhythm of heart internally in your entire body, everything, feet, legs, genitals, anus, waist, stomach, chest, arms, hands, fingers, neck, head, eyes, ears.

It will take a time, and probably several nights, sometimes, you can feel at all times the throb, for this it is important to control your mind, when you are inside you, when you are outside you, otherwise you will perceive it all the time, and it will be somewhat uncomfortable. Learn to recognize when you enter and when you leave yourself.

By having awareness that you can perceive your throb in any part of your body and at will, and at any place or time, you will begin to control your heart rate with your mind, faster, slower, feel your heart directly.

By doing so, you will also learn to control your temperature, colder, warmer. Repeat it all the time, and when you are sure you control it, look for the propitious night and prepare yourself.

Remember, to control your heart rate it is important to control your breathing, as long as this is done you can produce this state instantaneously. This is important to do so; it is the only way that exists to control your mind and spirit, when you begin to perceive the power.

## Night of initiation

While lying down, relax deeply; repeat in your mind ... the following words ...

**Prajna, Prajapati, Puruscha**
***Master of wisdom, reveal me the power of "BEING"***

They are the only human words that have some relation with those written on the stones of the dark door.

Overcome your fear, avoid getting out of control, remember, control, domination, control with your mind.

> ***I*** *(Say your name)* **invoke you secret power**
> **I freely enter the dark world**
> **I seek the secret of Mammon,**
> **I invoke the mysterious shadows of destiny...**

During this moment, learn to control with your breathing your heart rate, it is very important you learn to control your emotions, that you can have control over the unknown, when something strange appears or show up, first altering is your cardio-respiratory rate, and therefore you lose control of your thinking.

This loss of control leads to panic; it will be also very helpful in your daily life.

While in this state, perform the following, feeling your  heart rate within your hands, move one hand toward the other, as if you were going to pray, but without the palms touch.

According to your concentration, you will receive an energy field, it is not heat, it is your magnetism, perceive, know it, learn to feel, on having identified it through your mind take your throb all over your body, through all your skin feel the energy, project it, flow and feel as it expands, at the same time, perceive the sensations of the environment, develop your extrasensory perception.

To activate this sensitivity process allows you to identify the different entities of the shadows when they appear. Finished with the above, think about the situations of your life, everything is a test and everything you can control and change, you have initiated a new stage of your life.

## Exercises

• Get several male or female friends, try the following: ask them to place the hands with the palms up, move your hands closer and perceive the emanation of their energy. If you concentrate enough you can perceive in your body what goes on in that person's body.

• When you learn to feel and to perceive energy, close your eyes, place your hands palms up and ask the person to approach the hand to any of your hands, you will perceive in which one energy is.

Try it several times until it becomes something natural.

Then, approach a person, without having any contact, just get closer, feel his energy, his aura, and try to transmit or "touch" energetically to that person.

Try to think about a simple action, that he touch his hair, to look at you, to perform an action. Slowly you will begin to energetically affect everyone around you.

It is important, and if possible, buy a pet, a little dog, almost newborn, you will train and dominate your dog without words, only with your energy, show him what you want, avoid talking, just think when you think your vibration will transmit that desire that is captured by the dog, until you dominate it.

We have already seen the bodily energy or magnetism, as well as the control of the heart rate; let us now advance to the mental part.

Every thought is energy; it must be projected or received, for this is the training.

Please follow the steps below, first read the topic and then implement the experience.

For this exercise it is required concentration and serenity.

To start for a moment close your eyes, again, but this time place the hand in front of your eyelids, moving the hand you can perceive the difference between more or less light.

A kind of curtain appears, where you perceive the difference between clarity and darkness.

When you close your eyes, you will contemplate that curtain, but, mentally think about a color that you freely wish, you will perceive that a very tenuous point appears, through your mental concentration and serenity, cover all curtain with that color.

Then change the colors, until you achieve perceive the purple color. When it is easy to get it, focus on the farthest center of color, slowly you will perceive a series of shadows that form rings that come toward you or get out of you.

Begin to control the rings at your will, they come or go, fast or slow. In doing so keep in mind that you project your thinking when the rings come, that means you are going ... or leaving ... when the rings come out of you, you receive or perceive, please do not rush to send thoughts or wishes so quickly ... go step by step. These practices in Satanism required years.

Pretend that it is a tunnel with lights, if you go the lights come towards you; if you go back up the lights get out of you.

You are now in possession of the mental and physical techniques of control, it is required to practice every night to dominate the feelings, before venturing into the rituals of power.

# POWERS AND ELEMENTS

Everything that exists is composed by the elements Earth, Air, Water and Fire. With what you've learned, it's time to unify with the vibration of these elements.

Nothing better than to resort to nature, perceive the vibration of each one, go out, experiment, look, feel, smell, remember to search the essences, not the forms.

Identify your own code, there is no one that is universal, each person is a different vibration and perceives differently.

In doing so, now transport those feelings to the mental plane, create in your mind the same elements, but transform them, colors, shapes, aromas, etc., now according to the rings of your mind, project them, alter your environment by creating something new.

A warning, or suggestion, at the beginning while you tune your mind and your desire, will occur outdated events, imagine a candle and melt the battery of your car, or try something with the air and a window breaks, it usually happens, until you manages to canalize your mind.

The only suggestion is practice and practice and practice.

Although your desire to do and obtain things leads you to lose this type of practice, I would remind you that there is no genius in a lamp that does things for you, learning is not less than six years. That's why very few achieve it.

If you want wonders, it is better to do a theatrical illusion course, otherwise it is your power and for that time is required.

In fact, 7.000 years have elapsed and few ones even know it.

With this clear, let us open the doors of the underworld.

# DREAMS

The door of the underworld is the total conception of energy, spirit, soul that exist in all things and all things inside that primary energy.

In Satanism it is important to recognize that both the thought and the environment are similar in their essence, therefore, alterable, life and all its events are strange dreams where everything is susceptible to change if there is a change of consciousness and this essential quality is understood.

The ability to create an event in the mind, is the same ability that this event occurs in the material world, power is not only of god, anyone with a little bit of concentration and total freedom of spirit can do it.

**Beginning to act**
**Witchcraft or power**

To change or to influence something, first it is necessary to imagine what it is wanted to create, for that the mental image must possess the power, the anger, the desire, the passion are useless, while more subtle and seren is the mental image, more power you will have.

The Satanist in his beginnings needs a place, a series of elements that allow him to increase his concentration, a temple where he can delve into his knowledge, either alone or in a group, he concentrates his mind in "seeing" what he desires ... as in the technique of joining with the elements, so he must see the sequences in his mind.

• Can you imagine a flower opening from a bud?
• Can you imagine the aroma of burning wood?
• Can you imagine a candle with the black flame?
• Can you imagine these elements while reading these lines?

Without imagination there is no power ... you must begin to practice until you achieve it, who can not imagine is similar with the seagull whose wings are covered and it forget that can fly, who can not imagine is because his mind has been tied.

When you imagine, the image must come out through the rings of thought, without hesitation, without distrusting, without supposing, it is simply decreed, but do not try extravagant things at the beginning, like everything, start step by step ... When you want something for you ... you must imagine that you get it.

"Matthew 21

18 And in the morning returning to the city, he was hungry.

19 And when he saw a fig tree near the roady, he came to it, and he did not find anything in it, but only leaves, and he said to it: "Never again forever shall fruit come from you.

And then the fig tree dried.


20 And when the disciples saw it, they wondered said: how did the fig tree dry up?

21 And answering Jesus said to them: **Certainty I say to you, that, if you will have faith, and you will not doubt, you will do not only this of the fig tree but if you would say to this mountain: Take off and cast yourself into the sea, it will be done.**

**22And whatever you ask in prayer, believing, you will receive it."**


Satanism is power in freedom, manipulation of the church added to the plagiarism of the great teachings, but nullifying the power, saying ... AND EVERYTHING FOR WHAT YOU WILL ASK IN PRAYER ... but first it let be seen that the power is not from prayer but from each one ... Truly I say to you, that, if you have faith, and you will not doubt ...


So, it is not the prayer, that is the distraction to pay more tithes, it is self-confidence without hesitation in what you imagine, now well, what is more easier, to curse a fig tree that dries or that the other day it will give fruits, so ... that is not so easy, we have to wait for the harvest.

This kind of demonstrations is not worth, it is possible and you will try it.

We are going to do an experience, very interesting about the power that you possess, for that we need cooked rice, three clean and dry bottles.

In the three we place cooked rice, cold, exactly equal ... we mark one like neutral or of control, the second hate and contempt, the third one, love and power.

We leave the bottle of control far from others two, those of hate and love in different places... as you was who packed the rice, you know which one is which... now let's work.

Without being in front of the bottles think about them with the feeling they inspire you, those of control, take it out of your mental plane, but those of hate radiate it with hate; those of love, radiate it with love.

Wait fifteen days, you must start the experiment at full moon night ... and then look at the bottles ... avoid observing them during the days when it influences, but it is apporpiate to take notes, the time that each one influences, always avoid acting over the control bottle, at the beginning it is always unintentionally damaged.

Then observe what happened with the rice, and so that you trust a little more that you have the power, repeat the experiment as many times as you want ...

Let's play a little ... when do they attend to you poorly in a restaurant, do you began to discuss with the waiter? There is something easier ... do with all the meal the same made with the rice ... if you trust in you ... that you can ... well ... the restaurant must become nicer.

This is the same with plants and everything, but it is foolish to kill fish, damage flowers or fig trees for a demonstration of your power.

Do you like liquor?
When you're with your friends, look at the liquor no matter what it is, it's more effective with the beer ... frothy, remember the feeling of hate with the rice, just look at the beer and cut it ... at least you'll have a little fun... There is a sick person ... think about love of rice

and irradiate it ... who said that all satanism is only to destroy.

This entire universe is a dream, an energy that your mind can alter on condition that you trust in you. It is not a label of god or devil, it is your power and you can.

With these experiences, now is the time to go up in level, how much do you weigh? Imagine you with five kilos less, give an order to your body, and do a little sport you will see the results. **Warning!** Influencing the destiny of another human being or another living being is your responsibility, remember you take this power to the light or to the darkness, this treaty is only to be used personally for your benefit, if you act on another person, you unleash a world of energies that will eventually destroy you ...

# VISION OF THE FUTURE

In the first door of the underworld there is the world of dreams, in that universe the past, present and future time is caught in the same instant, on having developed the sensibility and power to create, something strange things happen, you will see the future or you will create the future, you will never know it. But it will happen.

Some images of future events or past to your mind will begin to arrive, either as images or sensations or hunches, the issue is that sometimes some images may be subconscious desires that create an event, which then you assume as a vision of the future.

Let's return with the experience of the energy of the hands or perception, now use the technique to identify the different vibrations according to the mood of those around you, do not think, do not try to create an image, allow the images to arrive, you will notice that perceive the emotions and can sense what is happening to that person.

In the same way, you learn to influence with your mind by changing moods, they are not words, they are mental images and energy.

# The Dark Side

Something terrifying can seem the next section in the world of Satanism, life and death are a sequence of the same event wrapped in two ends of eternity.

But you must wander in cemeteries at different hours, dawn, evening and night, it is important that you learn to feel the vibration and the characteristic smell of death. In this way the ghosts or the disembodied entities can be identified so not to confuse them with other entities of the shadows.

It isn't a game... this must be done responsibly, being more sensitive, you can obtain information about the "psychic echo" left on this plane by disembodied beings, this will be very helpful in your life.

Also you will feel and you will anticipate the presence of the death, both those who left and those who will leave, when death will come, days before a series of events or events, in the case of collective deaths for disasters, it comes that wave or signal, which will make your energy vibrate, for that you must go to the cemeteries and feel the presence of death, identify that specific code that reveals it.

Under your responsibility, you will slowly discover how to make pacts with that energy, and obviously it is only your responsibility what you want to do with that knowledge, but as a suggestion, do not ignore to identify this type of energies that can be very helpful in the future.

The first thing you should do on having finished this section is to change your lifestyle, to be better, to look better, to have and to increase your dignity, to control your emotions, to avoid being disturbed by trivialities, remember everything is a dream and you control that dream, when entering the world of wisdom, the magical essence of life will attract towards you many problems, many difficult situations, many disappointments, many bitter moments, and much pain, do not worry, it's the only way to train.

But you are free to take all those events as a punishment or bad luck or understand that you are an initiate in the power and the only way to understand how it works, is living experiences no matter how hard they are since you know they are not real.

Everything is energy, everything can be changed, and everything can be transformed.

*"The wise person to measurements, recognizing the relative unreality of the universe, imagines that he can defy its laws. That is nothing more than a silly and presumptuous, he will crash against the rocks and will be squashed by the elements, because of his madness".*

It is complex, extensive, to transcribe into a single book, which in itself is an arduous task, the concept of Satan, he is on earth the same time than god, and it is so little really what has been written on this topic, enter with the pacts, rituals, invocations of entities, spirits, seals, symbols, all the magical content of the old religion or witchcraft, spells and others that is an implicit part of Satanism, it would get a manual very difficult to understand.

For this reason this is the beginning of the power, the cornerstone, other complementary topics can be obtained in different books of ***Wicca la Escuela de la Magia [Wicca, the school of magic]***

# WISDOM FOR INITIATES

To enter to rediscover the ancient philosophical concepts of mental development is to venture into the understanding of the universe through meditation and maieutics, ancient cultures and ruminations showed a different knowledge about the constitution of matter, as well as the immanent force of thought.

When entering into Satanism, Wicca or primary religion we cannot separate ourselves from the physical and mental development of what exists, returning to ancestral explanations hidden in enigmas, we travel in time to understand the latent forces of the human spirit.

The religious conception imposed for centuries limited the knowledge leading humanity to the era of obscurantism. Today, fortunately, a new awakening in ancient knowledge is achieved.

Getting to understand the power of thought and the power of the spirit is an adventure, if you are prepared to find in these pages a path to enter the amazing universe of your wisdom.

In the Middle Ages (5th to 15th centuries), lived a strange subject, magician, wizard, sorcerer or enchantress, it is not really known; well-known as the magician Merlin, strange man; with very deep knowledge about Alchemy and magic, mysterious sciences in which it was supposed that transmutation of vulgar metals into gold was achieved, but unlike the magician achieved to materialize what he wanted, the same that to alter all his environment, to appear among the multitude or to disappear, he was friend and guide of King Arthur and the cavaliers of the round table, nobody ever knew about his birth and much less about his death.

But... did he really disappear... or... does he still appear occasionally...?

One day talking to him, thousands of years ago or yesterday, I saw him telling a story when he taught. It was recorded in my mind the peculiar style with which he started that I'm going to transmit it, in the same way I have to clarify that Christ: magician, witch, sorcerer or enchantress really nobody know, he also said something similar; but at their times to speak of these subjects was synonymous of death, and without contemplations one was sentenced to the bonfire or the cross, since some depraved people considered this knowledge as heresy.

Merlin said that in a place that is here and now, there is a very beautiful glass house, it has many rooms and many mirrors that do not reflect the image but they reflect the soul, and there all the acts are seen.

This mansion is something strange, to the bottom there is a stair that goes up a few steps and then go down to go back up again, something like go up going down, and go down going up, you can enter with the body or without it, you are down but up and you change at every instant.

Up and down, at the end and at the beginning of the stair there is a room full of dark light that shines without shine leaving everything in the darkness of the strange light, being able to see the invisible that everyone sees, walking without walking only being and standing you reach the door that won't open and never close, inside it being out of it, there is a bedroom without floor, nor ceiling, nor window, nor door and in the middle of the bedroom where there is nothing, is the table that has no legs or plank but holds a book, it has no pages, but list their sheets could never be, the pages are infinite and there all the wisdom of the world guarded by a golden owl that is nothing, its feathers are of air, its body from nothing, its beaks and eyes that are its beak and eyes are not, but being they see without seeing.

Only the one who is like owl can read the book that it does not exist, that is not seen in the crystal box that is here and now; this is the magic of the power to create.

You should explain it to you, so you will learn the magic of creation.

# PRINCIPLES OF THE HERMETIC PHILOSOPHY

## PRINCIPLE OF MENTALISM

**"Everything is mind the universe is mental"**

## PRIMARY ENERGY

Can you imagine a sunset? Well; we cannot define the energy that formed that image in your mind, but we can compare it with the first manifestation of energy of Everything.

Let's define it as "spirit" for not to be confused with all energy groups.

The spirit, in its first state, must have been of absolute rest, unalterable and unchangeable. Constant in itself, the initial stillness that still remains with the difference that it attracts towards itself. Which is the reason of this attraction?

The constant rest slowly attracts the energy towards its center, condensing it at its most infinitesimal point, doing so it is liberated inside itself towards your own interior.

The spirit in the absolute rest being without being, contracts itself since it is only in its own essence. Let's imagine a spiral or a fractal growing inwards itself in an infinite. They repeat themselves or copy their interiors in different and infinite scales.

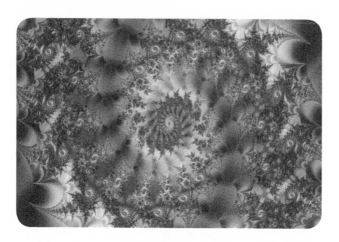

The harmony of the own rest makes that, in its stillness, spirit wrap in its own essence.

**Example:** if we take a laser beam and we send it to the space, we would assume that it would stay in a straight line: but not. There comes a time when it will begin to curve by its own weight, over itself until to join forming a circle, the circle may be quite wide and last a long time at the light speed to begin to attract. But the spirit has a difference, for it there is no space or time.

This movement (if we can call it that) or first impulse towards itself generates a change in the stillness, the process would be of condensation, let's take the previous example, if our laser beam had all the strength and the time would not be a line if not It would end up being a sphere generated by itself.

Similarly there would be two processes, one of attraction towards it, and the other of repulsion from its interior.

A passage of current 1 = attraction
A no passage 0= repulsion

The constant condensation would form specific accumulations as we saw in the first section, keeping the implicit initial matter, which in this condensation of attraction and repulsion, would form a specific magnetism + and – and although being the same essence they would be separated by this first attraction, the spirit would not be altered by this, it would be similar to imagine that it is day, when it is night, when it would happen, everything would dissolve again in the initial stillness; but for the spirit it would not happen like that, since it does not necessarily have desires, but for the energy of attraction and repulsion it should be harmonized until merging again without the existing polarity or perpetual repose of the spirit. In other words, nothingness would be Everything, when that Everything is dissolved, it would be essence with knowledge of "Being" according to how many subdivisions of attraction and repulsion have existed.

Now well, this attraction and repulsion would form certain condensations which should be triads, a positive, a negative and a neutral, if not, a pole would absorb the other being annulled the sequence, it is similar to two magnets where opposite poles are attracted and equal poles are repelled, but if it would lack poles or they attract totally or repel more, they would not be in equilibrium, which will be compressed more and more by its own strength.

The espíritu is slightly similar but for it there is no outside (it is everything) the only way that would be its own inner self compressing itself every time, but already with the essence of everything that exists, that internalization process will give as a logical consequence an externalization process, an attraction followed by a repulsion these two forces being equal complement the energy of the spirit, forming the triad previously seen.

The spirit, with its first mutation, the triangle of hermetic philosophy, one essence and two poles, would initiate a constant process of attraction and repulsion, but everything towards its interior, in this way, any creation would be inside the spirit, but varying in the quantity of attractions and repulsions.

Let's go back to the beginning where we talk about 0 and 1 is the same principle, let's take 0 as repulsion and 1 as attraction: How many combinations could we do? Infinite, right?, considering that the energy of the spirit is unlimited, something similar with what happens nowadays with computers that work in the same way, but being triads formed from the beginning + - + they could not be joined since on having be attracted in the

178

center, simultaneously they repel themselves, being all of equal loads they would remain in a balance rotating around the central axis. We have one (-) negative and two positive (++), the negative crosses them equally + - + and it would reach a point where the repulsion force of two positives wouldn't let them join to the negative one, these opposing forces would create a kind of constant gravitation staying in orbit, forming more groups of several +-+-+-+-, etc.; it can happen that ++ join together being higher their capacity of attraction but also could join together two - - keeping the balance, if it were not so nothing would exist, this process of + positives and - negatives, we will call it mind as computers do, later this condensed energy between positive and negative would form the basis of matter, based on the first element and we know hydrogen, which is nothing more than energy accumulation.

Growth, Hydrogen, Beryllium, Lithium] Everything only energy.

All other existing elements are based on H, like any other material cluster, (planets, constellations, atoms, etc.).

And everything absolutely everything material, would be contained in the spiritual and this in turn would be the primary energy constitution of matter.

The atom of H has the constant knowledge between its attraction and repulsion to stay like hydrogen, when attracting another series of charges changes gaining protons initiating a chain of infinite number of possible combinations, which when merged generate clusters that we could call molecules that integrated by association and adaptation become cells and these in turn become organisms, bodies, etc., by adaptation they unite conforming in harmony the own matter, plus any material group would have a "mind" for "be".

There is no difference between life and death, everything is alive; in a continuous adaptation and constant association in a cyclical way, day, night, day again, always travelling towards improvement or development of more perfect forms less matter, but greater energetic knowledge.

For a moment think about this, the earth, this planet are a compendium of many materials, they have implicitly all that man can discover or create in the future, in fact, the most advanced technology, is nothing more than modified mud. And all that exists will be again only mud, but the mental essence will have gained invaluable knowledge.

**Let's see an example:**

A few years ago a very rudimentary computer was the size of several rooms, today the technology goes in the same direction, less matter, but greater capacity, the old and gigantic computer, today is only a micro chip, which is associated to others forming a very sophisticated computing device, just as it happens in life, it advances towards an energetic perfection through matter which is energy, this apparent "evolution" returns to its beginning but with a greater accumulation of information and wisdom.

The matter is only a vehicle where the mind combines and assimilates the greatest quantity of information, regardless of how this knowledge is obtained, I mean: for the mind doesn't care the place or the way of acquiring knowledge, but only the own knowledge.

A computer chip dpesnt mind in what laboratory it was built.

And all knowledges are locked into a single function 0 -1 or negative (-) and positive (+).

The initial and substantial base of everything existing is the same that forms the mental state being it changeable through volitional processes, formerly this art was known as Alchemy.

The mind and the matter are changeable and transformable in accordance with the laws that govern them, the spirit is perpetual and unalterable, nothing can change it or modify it, nor itself.

The mind, being part of the large primary energy has the power to change itself and change the material environment, through a volitional attitude of projection, therefore is prudent to know that the mind is a different spirit apart but it is the own spirit.

The conception of an interior Everything is developed in the union of the planes, spiritual, mental and physical, being the essence that hides behind all the material forms, unalterable very few times it is perceived when contemplating the material form, one goes from seeing the substantial essence of being, the primary energy that makes everything that exists.

Let's see a tree. Not its fibers, nor its cells, nor its atoms.

If we make an analysis of anything that surrounds us, we will quickly realize that it is still an agglomeration of the first energy.

Let's take at random a mountain; the first vision is that of an accumulation of ground.

But let's look more closely at, what do we see? That the compound of this great mountain is made up of small particles of rock and earth, we use a magnifying lens, we see that these particles are made up of elements, small molecules which are composed by atoms, these in turn by a primary energy.

It may be that when speaking about an inner creation, it conflicts with some previously imposed concepts; we see apparently an expanding world.

Similarly, we contemplate that the vast majority of beings are born from a first point and grow out of themselves, through cellular associations, has been believed the hypothesis of the big-bang, a world in expansion that apparently grows out of its own center.

The apparent circumstances, from our point of view, can show us this event as real, but a series of questions that can hardly be answered are presented, if the absolute energy is in Everything and everything is immanent in the first substance, it could not be divided, outside it, it could not be added to itself without merge, or multiply and less diminish, it would be an unalterable, immutable and indefinable unit, it would have no time or space, it would have all times and all spaces, it would be nothing and it would be absolutely Everything, it could not create out itself, it could generate more inward its own worlds, universes, people, etc. (Later we will see the form of generation of primary energy).

This conception is too old, you can not really know when it was promulgated, the egocentric sense and concept degenerated into pseudo religions, which came into conflict with the principle of interior creation, from there one looks for an external god, which may not exist. Hypotheses of division and separation of the first energy have been taken, being individual to the subsequent generations.

# APEX

**Do you know what the apex is?**

Let's take a tour at the beginning of life, contemplating the sky, the galaxies, simultaneously contemplating the microcosm, something was found that powerfully attracted the attention of scientists, all atoms and planets have an inclination, this made us think about some physical alteration, but the apex theory was postulated, it consists in that all the material elements floating in the space and atoms point to a place lost in infinity, this is called the apex.

Now well, if that is the case, the question: What does exist beyond that apex or initial point at which the primary energy was concentrated to liberate the universe as we know it?

Well, according to the philosophy the immanent concept of the Everything, is in the creation towards its inward, which gives as a result the principle of the mentalism that says "Everything is mind and the universe is mental", not the mind of man but the mind of the Everything, this means that we are immersed in the central point of the infinite mind, it may seem that the universe is expanding, but actually it just merges inside the everything.

All that exists is immersed in the spirit energy, and all that exists is constituted by this energy. What tells us that we are implicit in the primary energy and thus even if we die we cannot living outside of it.

Let's see an example to better understand the relationship of Everything in all. Let's suppose that a person loses in an accident, his arms, his legs, his body completely, only remains his brain supported by artificial life and through it, the mind. This subject could create, generate a something; if so, coud you think for a moment how he would do it, taking into account that the brain cannot be multiplied, it cannot be divided, it cannot be enlarged. How would he create?

Maybe we think that, in these conditions, he could not create absolutely anything that couldn't justified to have him alive.

But if we think well, we would find that he can generate and create everything he wants, things, places, worlds as real as he would like, worlds with millions and millions of people, like you or me, being all of them the essence of himself and if any of them would die, in that sub-created world, the energy that created him, could not judge him, or condemn him, it would take him to nest in another being, in another form, in another creation so him would be absolutely with all, the energy of that thought would be multiform, the same force that would be used to create a man would be the same to create a galaxy and the moment when it would transform it, it will be done; everything would be controlled by the initial thought.

But what would happen if the first thought of that brain will generate a form, will leave it free without its control, only so that it will self-develop by itself; that form created by that thought would be a part of the thought, it would have the knowledge of the same thought, it would be exactly the same as the thought, we could think that it is a smaller part or equal to it, but it would never be itself, (it is already an independent energy). Then, if you have the same knowledge, towards where would you create it? Inward yourself.

Just as our brain, but without a body, would create towards its own center, towards its deepest part, so also its creations would enervate within itself, and everything simultaneously would live in that thought, even if they had different shapes and different occupations. If a sub creation of the sub creation, of the sub creation, better, if a creation of that smaller thought by comparing constellations, galaxies, planets, "men", could die in that thought, what would happen? The form as such of man would be erased from that thought, what that man has done, his psychic energy would remain with the knowledge without identity and would be elevated or joined to the energy of the thought that formed him, the energy would take that part of itself that which has taken more knowledge about it (which is the same of the great thought) and would put it again in another "form" to continue, the thought self knowing itself, since it could be projected in millions of ways, each form would have to release the knowledge that is implicit in it and in spite of having it, it is the general knowledge of the great thought.

Then, each form would not learn anything, it would know everything, it would be like a video projector, even if everything is on the tape you have to let it run to understand it, this way one should live and face different situations, to see and know how much knowledge one have inside, if it becomes more deeper, one would find that have all the knowledge and could also generate smaller forms and so on to infinity. How could you measure the time and size of those forms created inside that brain? We would talk about a subjective time, and it would be the time and the relative space, only for the created forms, a second could be equal to a thousand years, an atom to a galaxy, or also the inverse, 1000 years a second, a galaxy an atom, etc. What it would be for us that we observe that brain in a minute there would have existed galaxies, millions of worlds, planets, people, etc. Now, if some form should died, whatever it was and in the conditions that were except "self eliminating itself", would it die really?

No, it would not die, it would only would change form without matter the previous form or the experiences it had; that would remain as the psychic energy in that time-space in which that form lived; moreover, that energy after be released could join to another and those two form a better form; then no other form could have communication with the past of any and not with the future, since it being inside that brain time and relative space, there would be no past or future, but an eternal present.

Thus, a liberated form of the thought energy, becomes another form in a earlier or minor time, it will reincarnate in the past or in the future (seen from the point of time in the form), but even past and future would be a single present for the thought; but if a form is self-eliminating, doing so it would initiate a process in which it would annul the development of many forms since in all them they would be chained in the development of the thought of the brain of our imaginary experience; if this would happen, the thought would be altered by encapsulating the energy with the suicide pathogen on one side, so that it can not infest the others and there would be no opportunity to remain in form until the primary thought would vanish completely; in that brain, the apparent decease of any form of thought would only matter to the forms that are "alive", but to the base thinking, it would not really matter, since for it no form could truly die.

Now, how would the forms be created? That brain not having a physical body, it would have it mentally and not one body but millions, but we go slowly.

The first thought would produce an energy, if it is going to create, it would not create the form at once, but a concentrated energy that would have the ability to multiply through a process of attraction and repulsion, thus allowing different forms of association or better condensation of force and then liberation of millions of particles; those particles are unified in association forming many bodies, so until ending up being any quantity of forms, which would concentrate many forms of themselves, thus we would obtain worlds, galaxies, planets, beings, as soon as to the first forms of associating in different groups freedom is allowed; let us return for a moment to the part of chemistry, hydrogen and all its possible combinations to form all the chemical elements that we know; thus, the possible combinations among all these elements, if we analyze chemically a man and a planet, we see that in chemical constitution they are equal, the only difference would be in quantity and form.

As we have seen, a thought can internally create everything you want. How do we identify the energy that formed the primary thought? Not the chemical energy of the neurons, but the form, the thought; we could not define it by physics as we know it because neurons, and even the same brain is constituted with that same energy likewise the body, the man, the galaxies, the planets, the universe, the protons, the atoms, the molecules, etc.

Like in the example of the brain, we also extract the knowledge of ourselves; let us remember that each one is in itself a whole that absolute knowledge is in ouselves.

Now maybe we can better understand what the spirit really is. The energy that creates within itself, a pure energy that only in the calm of itself, generates a single force of attraction towards its interior, this attraction is condensed by becoming stronger until it explodes within itself; the repulsion comes; the positive and the negative, this polarity starts the process again by concentrating and expanding itself; there begin to act three energies, which we know like spiritual energy or absolute energy of all that is, mental energy or knowledge of pure polarity that something has; and physical energy which is the union of the spiritual and the mental in a single form.

At the end when the brain dies physically, it is difficult to know if the energy of thought with all its forms, worlds and universes continue living in another dimension.

Probably yes, the mind can live without a brain; something very similar happens with the spirit, being the energy that makes up all that exists.

Thus, we cannot speak about "spirits" or individual energies; we must mention that there is a spirit which contains everything. If not, we would have to say that there is only one spirit that contains Everything.

If not, we would have necessarily to think not in a whole but in a large number of different spirits that would lead us to conclude that all those spirits would form a single one, by any side that is analyzed, will be concluded the same thing "(Everything)" that contains all.

Even if something dies, apparently it continues having its spirit, it will remain submerged in it, nothing can "get out" or abandon or move away from the spirit or primary energy.

The matter can be transformed, it can have different appearances, but it will never escape from the spirit.

Something very strange happens in the conception of the spirit, **the matter really exists!**

Let's remember a section of the Emerald table to understand it, it should be clarified that Hermes gave this explication.

Everything that exists is submerged in energy, but we can not think that each one possesses a different or individual energy, everything is creation of the first one; but it is not direct creation of the form as such, but an energy in freedom that by attraction and repulsion would be associated in more complex states until result in the different organisms which later would form bodies, galaxies, etc.

Let us think for a moment about electrical energy, it is rather similar to the power of thought.

*"And as all things come from one, through the mediation of one, so all things have their origin in this one thing by adaptation."*

And in the same way the statement of the "Master Archetype": *"All the power that was, is or will be is here and now!"*

If everything is primary spirit and energy, what does it really exist?

The spirit or primary energy is not out of each one, but quite the opposite is found deep inside each being, as an example, if any form of our brain would want to find

194

the first thought, where does it would look? Outside it? Or in its own interior?

So let's not seek wisdom outside, nor in heaven or on earth, but inside in the deepest of ourselves

**What master could teach the inward path if he has never walked it, if doing it he wouldn't know how to teach since he would be immersed in his own self discovery, he could only show the path for everyone to walk it. The only and true teacher is oneself.**

When you can find the way to the interior, you can simultaneously extract all things from the spiritual world.

The master Archetype says:

*"From the inexhaustible riches of its limitless substance, I extract all the necessary things, spiritual and material".*

We have Everything within us and we are free to have what we truly desire.

*"Although it is true that everything is in Everything, it it is not less than Everything is in all things. The one that understands this properly has acquired a big knowledge".* The Kybalion

After this section you can think if the life you live is the one that corresponded to you, or is the one you have created in your decision.

# PRINCIPLE OF CORRESPONDENCE

*"As above, so below; as below, so above."*

The hermetic principle that shows there is no difference in the extremes, regardless of their direction, tall, short, large, small, macro and micro, everything corresponds to everything, wealth and poverty.

Everything corresponds to another extreme on the scale, therefore, in the philosophy of Satanism, it is understood that on the scale of correspondence everything is to everything through the mental process, a cent is to wealth what an atom is to a galaxy, and in turn, the galaxy is an atom, and wealth a cent.

It depends solely and exclusively on what part of the scale is between the macro and the micro.

Now something that must be understood and applied, correspondences occur among specific essences, love does not correspond with wealth, remember, at the moment of creation everything has a specific "mind" of being.

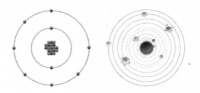

The atom of Fluorine, with nine electrons, is a micro representation of our solar system, micro and macro, the two are essentially the same, wanting to influence one or the other, it will depend on the direction towards where it goes, macro cosmic or micro cosmic, the size is a perception of your size in relation, but in Satanism that size is relative, so if you imagine yourself as a giant, the solar system will be an atom, if you imagine yourself being an infinitesimal being, the atom will be a system.

It depends solely on your mental position, this acts on everything, or you grow or minimize yourself in different situations.

Thus, the intiate understands that each event of his life has implicitly two extremes on the scale, that depends on his freedom in which degrees of the scale he acts and which one he wants to change, but it is important in this part to recognize the action of the law of reversed effect, while more travel to one extreme more abandone the other one, obtaining the opposite of what is desired. In applying this principle, it is possible to understand the events that form the creation or association that produces growth.

This principle applies to all situations of life, but before it is necessary to understand the following ones that in they compose a whole.

# PRINCIPLE OF VIBRATION

*"Nothing is immobile; everything moves; everything vibrates"*

The complex of Hermetic philosophy leads us to result on principles that do not act on their own, but they are intertwined in an infinite wheel, for such a motive it is suggested to the reader for his best comprensión, to follow the sequence, taking each part individually and each added principle as new information. In this way, each principle added to the previous generates a new concept.

This principle is the basis of the previous one, it is directly related to the movement of the scale between the macro and the micro, please focus your attention on understanding how this principle works.

*Let's interlace the foregoing:*

**Mentalism**, everything is mind and everything is created inside the infinite **mind** of the EVERYTHING, but it is created as energy or **spiritual plane**, in turn it associates and forms the three planes, **the matter** as we know it, from the micro to the macro, **the mind**, the code that is required for something to be.

**The correspondence**, everything corresponds between macro and micro, depending on its essence, up or down is the same, from the subtlest to the densest.

**Vibration**, in the scale of creation everything vibrates, everything obeys with a specific frequency, ranging from slow, quiet vibrations that have a cadence of million of eons, almost imperceptible even for the time, to vibrations whose intensity is so high and quickly that are not perceived.

It is important not to confuse with sound or light, it is the vibration of "Being" although both, sound and light are good examples.

This vibration is due to planes, mental, like knowledge, for example let's see atom again.

The hydrogen atom has a certain frequency of vibration  or movement to be a hydrogen atom, to remain as such and to continue like this.

Imagine the frequencies of the most recent discovery, the Teneso, and these in turn linked to other material elements, vibrate in infinite scales of change, without doubt there are more elements that science will discover in this material world.

This produces on the mental and physical plane, the mind also vibrates at different scales between a state of mental quietude or meditation or trance, up to a state of exaltation and fury.

The question how do you think the vibration of the spirit is, intense or subtle? Several answers, for this question, as essence it does not vibrate, is in a constant eternal quietude, when it starts the movement of the interior creation, the interior creation only alters the creation, not what contains it, it is just like the earth, we vibrate in different scales with everything that exists, but deep space remains in stillness.

All that exists vibrates, everything is variable and mutable, everything is changeable, and everything can be controlled, combined, altered, in this way, the art of knowing the different vibrations gives as a response the obtaining of power, if this principle is applied to everyday life are discovered the scales, the complements, the attractions and repulsions, as with magic and Satanism, to know the elements that unleash intense or subtle vibrations they give power and wisdom. Stones, plants, seasons, planetary phases, magnetism, mental states, emotions, diseases, health, wealth and poverty, success and failure, etc.

Vibration is in everything, mind acts on that vibration either the mental field, or the physical field, and do you remember the experience of rice?

*Let's interlace the foregoing:*

**Mentalism**, everything is mind and everything is created inside the infinite mind of the EVERYTHING, but it is created as energy or spiritual plane, in turn it associates and forms the three planes, the matter as we know it, from the micro to the macro, the mind, the code that is required for something to be.

**The correspondence**, everything corresponds between macro and micro, depending on its essence, up or down is the same, from the subtlest to the densest.

**Vibration**, in the scale of creation everything vibrates, everything obeys with a specific frequency, ranging from slow, quiet vibrations that have a cadence of million of eons, almost imperceptible even for the time, to vibrations whose intensity is so high and quickly that are not perceived.

It is important not to confuse with sound or light, it is the vibration of "Being" although both, sound and light are good examples.

# PRINCIPLE OF POLARITY

*"Everything is dual, everything has two poles, everything has its pair of opposites, like and unlike are the same; opposites are identical in nature, but different in degree; extremes meet; all truths are half-truths; all paradoxes may be reconciled".*

The universe, although "it is", it is also true that "it is not" everything would depend on the position with which one looks; if it is from the material plane, matter and the universe are real; from the mental everything is an illusion.

From the mental plane only the mind would exist, matter would be a thought or an illusion being unreal.

Everything is simultaneously absolute and relative in essence, but the absolute is given at the beginning, the rest is relative, outside of EVERYTHING in itself, what exists is relative nothing is "absolute" more than the union of Everything in Everything. Relative and absolute sometimes need a very deep meditative analysis to achieve their true understanding.

"Everything is simultaneously absolute and everything is simultaneously relative".

If we take love this would only be absolute like love implicit in the feeling, just as hate would also be absolute in feeling, but relative as love or hate.

The feeling is **absolute** regardless of whether it is love or hate, but love and hate are relative since there could not exist an absolute love or absolute hate. We will never know where the one ends and where the other begins.

Everything, absolutely everything, maintains this principle. As an example: the temperature being one has two extremes, cold at an extreme and heat on the other, being both at the same time, cold and heat; I mean, there is no an absolute cold, nor an absolute heat, but there is one temperature, even the most extensive cold is hot to the degree that follows it; example, 12 degrees, is more hot or less cold than 11 degrees; speaking about heat, as with cold is less hot than the one preceding it and superior than the one preceding it; we could not think about a total cold or total heat, we would only talk about temperature.

Let's observe the freedom, the freedom possesses two poles, extroversion and introversión, good or evil, to be or not to be, any extreme vibrates on the scale and therefore is polarized.

Everything has two poles, its two sides, except the spirit, everything that exists has that polarity two extremes in a balance, where they interact the correspondence of similar, the vibration of being and the other principles that follow, this is in order to associates mentally how the power works.

 Remember, you are who controls the balance of everything that exists and you place or remove the weights in the extreme you want.

Everything, although "it is", it is also true that it is not, this duality and triad, simultaneously they are one, in essence, each one is its respective vibration, it cannot be transmuted the temperature into feeling or turn the cold into love, although they remain intrinsically united, bound by time and space.

Let's analyze the divine paradox, a sentence of the Kybalion that will allow us to understand in a better way what concerns the relative.

*"The wise person at measures, recognizing the relative unreality of the universe, imagines that he can defy its laws. That is no more than a fool and presumptuous, who will crash against the rocks and he will be squashed by the elements, because of his madness".*

**For a moment a little imagination.**

By exposing that the world really is, but is also not, one enters in contradiction, let's look at something interesting, you believe that the world is real, because you feel it so, you see it, you sense it, you smell it, you perceive it, you observe your surroundings from the physical point that you are, but let's look at this.

The whole information that comes to your brain, are only electrical impulses, just as on a computer screen you can see everything, feel and perceive that what you see is real.

[Ghost effect, or energy of a cut leaf, using Kirlian photography]

There is no image, but you see images, there is no odor, but you perceives it, there are no colors, you think to see them, there is nothing ... only wave frequencies, everything you feel, see, perceive, smell, all their senses, are nerve terminals of electrochemical impulses, reality friend mine, if you could see the world as it really is, you only would see all the energy at different scales of vibration, more intense, more soft, there is nothing of what you think is real.

This is related to power dreams and paranormal events that every neophyte thinks can produce quickly, have the power of telekinesis, turn lead into gold, create supernatural portents, be invisible, make a snap with his fingers and something happens, no, it does not work this way the true Satanism, but if there is the possibility of achieving that and more, to reach that requires much learning and when it is obtained is understood that it is not worthwhile.

If you could do everything with your mind, whatever, what would be the meaning of your life?

Read carefully the following and you will understand

**The divine paradox**

*The real wise person knowing the nature of the universe uses the law against the laws: the superiors against the lower ones, and through the Alchemy it transmutes what is not desirable, in the valuable and this way he triumphs.*

*The adapted does not consist of abnormal dreams, visions or images, phantasmagoric, but in the wise use of the superior forces against the inferior forces, thus escaping from the pains of the lower planes vibrating in the higher ones. Transmutation, not presumptuous denial, is the weapon of the teacher."*

Let's remember once again, the extreme poles of the truth, the absolute and the relative, all truths contain the absolute and the relative, they are and they are not.

So we can not ignore any of the extremes, it is vital to analyze every circumstance from the two extremes, taking care to fall into absolute situations when they are really relative; we can not deny the matter nor the existence of the universes although we know that they are an illusion, we live caught inside that illusion, our brain, body, etc.; it is constituted by the same

elements that constitute the universes, but our mind not; this is so subtle that matter may not alter it.

More knowing the laws that govern this three-dimensionality it can transmute passing from one end to the other, we must understand each of these laws or principles to learn how is transmuted the negative into positive and on the contrary.

The world itself is only an instant for *the Absolute Everything*. But for us it is a reality and an illusion, being both real.

Caught in this time - space.

We cannot escape from the laws that govern us but we can alter and transmute, change the undesirable into the valuable.

For our physical body everything is real, we are an integral part of the material universe and despite it, we understand that it is an illusion. We cannot forget that we are living inside that era and its laws govern us. Trying to hit a wall will hurt us since the wall and our bodies vibrate in the matter, but for our mental body the wall, the body and the universes do not exist. But if you use intelligence and vibrate on the different scale of the wall instead of hitting it, you build a door. The human possesses that creative quality, the animals ram the wall.

*Let's interlace the foregoing:*

**Mentalism**, everything is mind and everything is created inside the infinite mind of the EVERYTHING, but it is created as energy or spiritual plane, in turn it associates and forms the three planes, the matter as we know it, from the micro to the macro, the mind, the code that is required for something to be.

**The correspondence**, everything corresponds between macro and micro, depending on its essence, up or down is the same, from the subtlest to the densest.

**Vibration**, in the scale of creation everything vibrates, everything obeys with a specific frequency, ranging from slow, quiet vibrations that have a cadence of million of eons, almost imperceptible even for the time, to vibrations whose intensity is so high and quickly that are not perceived.

It is important not to confuse with sound or light, it is the vibration of "Being" although both, sound and light are good examples.

**Polarity**, everything acts according to the law, it is formed, it is created, it corresponds, it vibrates and it has two poles, the ends of the subtlest vibrations. The mind is responsible for vibrate from one extreme or the other, the polarity exists in all its specific essence, all extrems are reconcilable, a very intense hate can be transformed in love and in turn love into hate.

# PRINCIPLE OF RHYTHM

"Everything ebbs and flows; everything has its avance and setback tides; all things rise and fall; everything moves like a pendulum; the measure of its swing to the right is the measure of its swing to the left; rhythm is the compensation."

With a quick view of the world that surrounds us we can define that everything has a cycle between one pole and another, everything is born and dies, everything is transformed into consecutive sequences, everything has an abb and flow, everything comes and goes, between two extremes, rhythm is the speed with which one goes from a minor degree to a major one or from one major to a minor one between correspondence, vibration and polarity, Rhythm, that soft mutation that occurs imperceptibly, some are natural, day and night, the presence and absence of the seasons that follow each other with all the natural changes that occur.

Rhythm that travels to one extreme then loses speed and returns, that movement compensates for not polarizing, however, when reaching an extreme without compensation, it is the same as a car that accelerates in a descent, the brake controls rhythm or speed, but if it is not applied ... inevitably everything goes back to zero, with a disaster.

To understand, everything moves between the two poles of ebb and flow, rhythm or speed in which it passes from one extreme to another is the "compensation" if the balance tilts to one side, it must compensate by placing weight on the other.

It is important to keep this in mind for all the acts of life, when the savings account is empty it is necessary fill it, there is no more, or poverty will come.

To take into account
• Every natural rhythm alters the mental rhythm.
• All extreme polarity transmutes the other extreme in a radical way.
• There cannot alter rhythms of different essences, cold love, wealth in health, only the equals are polarized.
• All rhythm can be modified in the mental plane, to be in summer, but to think about winter.
• The speed with which one actes to stop the rhythm is the beneficial compensation.

• Must learn to recognize the ebb and flow, or tides of changes, everything warns when it starts, stillness is the beginning.

• Every rhythm slows down and loses speed before changing.

• Everything is losing momentum when it reaches the critical point and the change starts, of continuing it will return to another extreme in a violent way.

• There is no flow without ebb.

• The rhythms act with own wisdom.

The reader is recommended to read the book *"Leyes de la Magia" [Laws of Magic]* to understand how they act different principles and different laws that govern them.

*Let's interlace the foregoing:*

**Mentalism**, everything is mind and everything is created inside the infinite mind of the EVERYTHING, but it is created as energy or spiritual plane, in turn it associates and forms the three planes, the matter as we know it, from the micro to the macro, the mind, the code that is required for something to be.

**The correspondence**, everything corresponds between macro and micro, depending on its essence, up or down is the same, from the subtlest to the densest.

**Vibration**, in the scale of creation everything vibrates, everything obeys with a specific frequency, ranging from slow, quiet vibrations that have a cadence of million of eons, almost imperceptible even for the time, to vibrations whose intensity is so high and quickly that are not perceived.

It is important not to confuse with sound or light, it is the vibration of "Being" although both, sound and light are good examples.

**Polarity**, everything acts according to the law, it is formed, it is created, it corresponds, it vibrates and it has two poles, the ends of the subtlest vibrations.

# PRINCIPLE OF CAUSE

*"Every cause generates causes, every cause obeys with the previous cause, everything happens in accordance with the Law; the luck is not more than the name with which an unknown Law is named; there are many levels of coincidence, but nothing escapes to the Law."*

We have heard every cause has an effect, but really the effect or fruit of an initial cause, inevitably is the beginning of a minimum of two other causes, without entering into controversy, but with a deep look of secrecy and creation, the only effect that could exist would be the end of all possible causes.

For this treatise on Satanism, I ignore the term **effect**, leaving it as continuity of causes, every effect generates two new causes, not two effects of the first cause, the original cause has mutated in two new causes and thus towards the infinite.

Nothing happens by chance, nothing happens by coincidental, everything is due to the process of creation, there is no a why there is only a for what, every event is the answer of millions of causes which, although not be known or identified, the sum of micro causes generates a macro cause, example:

Hypothetically let's think about the sea, we are going to divide it by the equator, half and half in complete quietude, in the south hemisphere, a whale jumps and creates a wave that breaks the stillness, that initial wave is a small cause, who smoothly alters the serenity of the sea, this small disturbance, over time will become a marine storm that will hit the northern hemisphere without know its initial cause, this storm generated other causes that ultimately destroyed the whale that begun all and so on continues the process generating more and more and more causes the sea more and more and more causes, the sea never more will return to the initial quietude, has been unchained, I clarify chaos not destruction.

This principle shows that everything happens for some reason, sometimes that reason is improbable to be recognized, the original cause, if you evaluate your life, you will find that you have caused some situations at a certain time.

Causes travel to different poles, but they can always be harmonized if one can handle the rhythm of the same ones.

Basically this principle answers many questions, thus, the Satanist understands that it must be creator of new causes and not be the servant of causes created by others.

In all events of life new causes can be generated, remember each new cause generates a minimum

of two causes that will continue to generate, even if the original cause has mutated.

It is complex to define if there could be the end of all causes, in the first impulse of the EVERYTHING on having generated within itself, each generation created already has become a whole EVERYTHING than the original EVERYTHING, as the EVERYTHING does not obey or have emotions or human laws it was, it is, and it will be ... forever. EVERYTHING is just the essential energy in absolute freedom.

*Let's interlace the foregoing:*

**Mentalism**, everything is mind and everything is created inside the infinite mind of the EVERYTHING, but it is created as energy or spiritual plane, in turn it associates and forms the three planes, the matter as we know it, from the micro to the macro, the mind, the code that is required for something to be.

**The correspondence**, everything corresponds between macro and micro, depending on its essence, up or down is the same, from the subtlest to the densest.

**Vibration**, in the scale of creation everything vibrates, everything obeys with a specific frequency, ranging from slow, quiet vibrations that have a cadence of million of eons, almost imperceptible even for the time, to vibrations whose intensity is so high and quickly that are not perceived.

It is important not to confuse with sound or light, it is the vibration of "Being" although both, sound and light are good examples.

**Polarity**, everything acts according to the law, it is formed, it is created, it corresponds, it vibrates and it has two poles, the ends of the subtlest vibrations.

**Rhythm**, everything is interrelated, creation is formed by association, in turn corresponds to macro and micro, which in turn vibrates at different scales and different planes, this vibration generates polarities, the passage from one pole to another is the rhythm, the speed of the rhythm is the compensation. The ebb and flow, the day following night, the handling of the mental rhythm is the key to transform the universe.

**Causation**, a great principle that continues integrating the previous ones, everything obeys an initial cause, any cause generates two causes, the created cause cannot change, every cause acts in time, rhythm marks the event, when the polarity stops with the rhythm a new cause is born.

# PRINCIPLE OF GENERATION

*"The generation exists everywhere; everything has its masculine and feminine principles; the generation is manifested at all levels".*

The last of the principles with which integrates the image of Baphomet and hermetism, the ANDROGYNOUS CREATOR.

Since the Mentalism, the creation advances, not the evolution, nothing evolves, the original cause mutates in other causes, both the mind and the matter generate, create, associate, as a kaleidoscope of life, the essence is in continuous creation.

Everything possesses the generating polarity, fertilization is not only at the gender level, in absence of a unique process of female-female or male-male, all enters in the androgynous female-male, still in the mental plane more ingrained is this principle.

The feminine side is gestator, the masculine side is fertilizer, it is important for the reader to take out of context the issue of sexual gender in this principle, in this part they all concur simultaneously with the previous principles, something that is important to take into account.

The principle of generation is the way by which the original cause of a particular event or material creation from the mental plane is created. It is the maximum secret of the Emerald table, in the maximum work of thought.

Remember that you must pay attention to the following section, you may get confused at the beginning, but if you've read the other  principles it'll be easy for you to understand this.

All of us somehow think about the art of "creating" just by thinking, producing a certain alteration, making a certain event happen, attracting or moving something away from our life, an unparalleled power that allow us to influence the universe obtaining a benefit or creating a wonder or a miracle.

We initially reject the idea like something improbable, or impossible, this possibility does not exist, but ... the truth is another.

You can attract or remove from your life what you want, many people do it involuntarily and naturally without knowing the acting principles, others, they perceive that power, when thinking about something, that something is obtained, but then they repeat it and fail.

The art of generating some of the energy of the universe lies with the ability to imagine what is desired. In fact, everything that exists materially and technologically speaking, has been created as a thought.

Everything is mind and the universe is mental.

Under the first principle of Alchemy, is the postulate that indicates that everything is energy and this energy is also in your mind. Remember the topic seen.

Now well, if we concentrate our mind in creating an image of something that is desired, it means that it already exists in the mental plane, but it must be projected onto the physical plane.

Here begins the matter to take life, now you should think about the principle of correspondence, **"As above is below"** the mental image of a certain vehicle is already on the mental plane, but it must be prudent, or it can attract the same car like a toy or a miniature, remember for energy there is no size, macro or micro is the same.

So you must be very clear in which correspondence you create that mental image, iqual this part in cases of difficult life events, you can turn a problem into something minimal or magnify it, in turn you can be seen as a giant warrior before the adversity, or you can be seen like a pygmy.

The same thing with everything that surrounds you, you take your mental power on the scale down, or up, meditate on this for a moment, there is no a problem, only unknown solutions, while you more minimize the problem, more solutions you will have.

Let's return with the example, the car that you imagine must vibrate, "Nothing is immobile, everything moves, everything vibrates" the car in the mental image must vibrate, the key is to "feel" it, to imagine it as real, to drive it mentally, to make it an integral part of that thought that must be intensely lived.

It comes from the nothingness of thought will materialize of the material world, it will be nothing in the mind, and it will be again, just mud. So look at what point between nothingness and matter you imagine it, used, damaged, broken, new; etc., that is the vibration that you must give to your mental creation, and equal with everything in your life, the end of a situation, the beginning of one, the scale of vibration is handled only by you.

**"Everything is dual, everything has two poles, everything has its pair of opposites, like and unlike are the same; opposites are identical in nature, but different in degree; extremes meet; all truths are half-truths; all paradoxes may be reconciled".**

Now think for a moment, what is the polarity of a car? Let's look at this in the principle of generation; everything has a feminine and a masculine part. Now, which is that of a car? The engine is the active or fertilizing part, body or form is the feminine part.

On having created where your mind goes, to the feminine part of the body the external

part; the form is attracted and subjugated by the external, sometimes the internal is ignored.

In the mental generation you must be careful in which part you polarize, both are equally important, it might have a body without engine and still in a body there are implied the two poles: one feminine and one masculine.

A comment, although there is an eagerness to do rituals and launch a pact with Satan, it is important to ventilate how the theme works, otherwise without knowledge, one falls into the believe by faith, this theme as old as humanity is worth explaining, even if it is a bit extensive, if you read it carefully you will understand how the power of mental polarity works and when you execute rituals to know the reason.

## MENTAL PLANE

There are thousands of treatises about mind, intelligence, personality, character, reason, consciousness, subconsciousness; etc., and undoubtedly this is another more, none has a unique truth, even today it cannot be defined what is the mind.

We suppose and it is supposed, that all these concepts obey with a nervous system, a network we call a brain, a gelatinous mass full of convolutions, where 86 000 000 000 neurons, approximately, but they can be many more.

Now, many animals have similar brains with certain quantities of neurons, the African elephant wins us, 267 000 000 000, almost four times more, and it does not have the capacity to create, much less to reason, although it shares with humans its attraction for death.

If we accept that the mind is product of a chemical exchange at the neuronal level, logically this event would occur in different species, but ... What does happen if the human mind is not a neurochemical reaction but an external energy?

This hipótesis takes force, in front of the continuous narratives of whom have lived through extracorpooreal experiences, or experiences outside the body, unfoldment, astral unfoldment, travelling conscience, psychic projection, tanatonauts, etc.

This psychological and neurological abnormality has existed since the dawn of humanity, rejected completely by science, but... If it is real as confirmed by those who have died, but they return to the life and narrate their extracorporeal experiences where they live intensely out of their dead body, but with the ability to retain information and remember what they has been lived extracorporally.

This allows us, within Satanism, to understand the mind as an external energy of the physical body or brain, but intrinsically linked to it, even dreams could be an extracorporeal experience.

If we take the postulates of alchemy everything is mind, our mind is something that is beyond a conglomeration of neurons.

We have two types of mind, two poles, two extremes.

**A conscious mind**

When making an analysis we find that the conscious part is that which fulfills the functions of the vigil with specific analyzes; let's see.

The conscious mind is in charge of controlling, analyzing, reasoning, quantifying, being objective, rejecting information that is not compatible, taking different alternatives, etc.

But the conscious mind does not create, does not have the capacity to create by generating, and less it imagines, it takes all the information from the accumulation of memories recorded in the subconscious.

The subconscious does not analyze, does not quantify, does not control, does not reason, is not objective, does not reject the information received, does not take alternatives, it believes absolutely everything, and it creates in the sense of generating through the only language it has: the imagination.

But it has the peculiarity that it never rests, it is always receiving information given by the senses or by extrasensorial way, even in the states of deep coma, even in the brain damage it continues taking information and generating information.

The unconscious which would be as one division more, would be the level where there would be no consciousness or subconscious, but that never happens, the use of this word is given more to identify non-consciousness, that to deny the status of the subconscious.

The real unconscious does not exist, nor a series of subdivisions created to analyze the neurocerebral capacity or the psychological attitude. We have an example of the conscience and the subconscious:

If we suggest to a man that roses are blue, the conscious mind analyzes the information, and after evaluating it according to his different memories, he rejects that information for not being compatible with the range of colors of the roses he has in his memory. But if we would say to the subconscious that roses are blue, the subconscious only generates it and delivers an image of a blue rose; the subconscious mind creates all the time and transmits that information to the conscious levels, even in waking state the language used by the mind is only through images and no words in any language, although it is repeated thousands of times it achieves to have some effect in its generating capacity.

From there the old Chinese adage; "A picture is worth a thousand words" that's why, if one repeats "I'm fine" those words by themselves do not have any effect, but if you see the image, the subconscious automatically generates that creation.

So we can understand, that our mind in that polarity generates and creates images, but must be fought with the control of consciousness, which leads with the doubt, the impossible, the improbable, the negation, the uncertainty, these mental processes of negation limit the power of the irradiated thought, that is why, the rituals and some prayers overcome the negation giving the power that is required.

The conscious mind controls everything, the subconscious mind "generates" everything, wealth, poverty, health, illness, love, hate, etc. It is important that the initiated knows and understands the laws that govern magical power.

When it's about to creating "something", that something must be in the subconscious ... every apprentice is trained in the art of controlling the mind, the negation of consciousness is the blockade of the subconscious, the imagination gives power, the conviction of the possible results in the materialization of the created.

When the image is generated and projected, it must be taken into account that everything has an ebb and flow, as in correspondence, the rhythm marks the time when something is desired to occur.

*"Everything flows and reflows flux; everything has its avance and setback tides; all things rise and fall; everything moves like a pendulum; the measure of its swing to the right is the measure of its swing to the left; rhythm is the compensation."*

It is your mind, your creation that places the image in a specific space-time, comes to you from the material world or leaves from you to the material world.

It cannot get anything that has not been created, so, you must pay attention to this part, the car you want will not be built from nothing, someone somewhere has already did it, otherwise you should plan and build it.

The mind "attracts" something that already exists, or imposes a psychic energy, "energy".

The principle of rhythm is of delicate handling, if something is desired with much impetus, the opposite is obtained or nothing is obtained. It is important to know when you want something to happen; otherwise it is an empty job that will not produce anything.

Everything ebbs and flows, is important to recognize the signs of change, and act in accordance with the times, and if you connect with the cosmic mind and project the car that you want, surely you must have that sent signal somehow will attract your desire to your life, but ... but you must also act, it will not appear in the entry door of your home. But yes, you will have all the facilities to obtain it. Beware of ebb, your mental creation if you take away yours strength, it will vanish. It is like money of chance and games, the old comment that says: "what comes by water, by water goes away".

*"Every cause generates causes, every cause obeys with the previous cause, and everything happens in accordance with the Law; the luck is not more than the name with which an unknown Law is named; there are many levels of coincidence, but nothing escapes to the Law."*

When creating a mental image, is due to a cause and it will generate from its creation many more causes that affect your whole environment, think how many situations are altered with the fact that you have a car, the manufacturer, the seller, your home, your neighbors, your world, the world of others, that ignored event moves the threads of the world, attracts causes generated by others and creates causes generated by you. In other words, your cause affects all causes by keeping them within the law or original cause.

All process created by the will, is strengthened by the power of the causes generated by others, therefore, your power will increase proportionately to the extent that generates more causes. As you can see, these principles acting simultaneously on the creation, generation, polarity of whatever you want, the hermetists, Satanists, vampires, and many more, have applied this knowledge from the beginning the church knowing the power, annulling it by demonizing it.

*Let's see the context of the philosophy of Baphomet.*

With everything you have just understood and read, I ask you to please think, analyze, observe, and understand the following sections.

# THE TRUTH ABOUT THE SELF THE ARCHETYPE MASTER

"The entire power that was, is or will be is here and now!"

1. I am a center of expression for Primary Will towards good that eternally creates and sustains the universe.

2. Through me, your unfallible wisdom takes form of thought and word.

3. Full of understanding of its perfect law, I am guided moment-to-moment along the path of liberation.

4. From the inexhaustible riches of its limitless substance, I extract all the necessary spiritual and material things.

5. I recognize the manifestation of the undeviating justice in all the circumstances of my life.

6. In all things great and small I see the beauty of divine expression.

7. Living from that will, sustained by its infallible wisdom and understanding, mine is the victorious life.

8. I hope confidently the perfect realization of the eternal splendor of unlimited light.

9. In thought, word and deed, I entrust my life, day by day, to the firm foundation of the Eternal Being.

10. The kingdom of the spirit is incorporated in my flesh."

# THE EMERALD TABLE OF HERMES

*"Truth, without falsehood, true and very true, what is above is like what is below and what is below is like what is above for the realization of the miracles of the One Thing. And since all things come from One, by the mediation of One, so all things have their origin in this One Thing by adaptation. The Sun is its father, the Moon its mother, the Wind takes it in its belly, and its nurse is the Earth. This is the father of all perfection, or consummation of the world. Its power is integral, if it is converted into earth.*

*You will separate the earth from fire, the subtle from the dense, gently and with great ingenuity. It ascends from earth to heaven and descends again to earth and receives the power of the superiors and the inferiors. Thus you will have the glory of the whole world; for this reasons all darkness will flee from you. This is the strong force of all forces, overcoming everything subtle and penetrating every solid thing. This is how the world was created. From here were all the wonderful adaptations, of which this is the way. For this I am called Hermes Trismegistus, having the three parts of the philosophy of the whole world. What I have to say is complete, concerning the operation of the Sun."*

Did you understand it? It is simple, it is mind, they are the principles acting, every word represents the form of **"mental creation".**

## The Kybalion

There is no real consensus, nor the meaning, nor when, nor who really is the author, that, obeys with the law of the cause, this ancient knowledge, applied, exposed by different philosophies almost always framed in the occultism, have been the basis of current religions.

The image of Baphomet is the icon representing the hermetic and initiatory wisdom in the domain of the laws that govern this universe, who apply them, study them, melts with them will dominate the world.

The following hermetic axioms are to meditate, to reflect and to understand the depths of this theme, in this book; it is only an appetizer, a subtle vision of the unlimited and infinite universe of mental magic.

239

I ask you please take time to read these comments, unify what was previously seen, and understand how you can apply them to your life and how they act.

# HERMETIC AXIOMS

• *"The possession of knowledge, if not accompanied by a demonstration and expression in practice and in the action, is the same as burying precious metals: a vain and useless thing. Knowledge, as well as fortune should be used. The law of use is universal, and that life is suffering for being in conflict with the forces of nature".*

• *"To change your characteristic or mental state, change your vibration".*

• *"To change a degree of undesirable vibration, act in the principle of rhythm, stop the flow of that undesirable polarity, in the ebb of the opposite pole. The undesirable is transmuted by changing its polarity towards the valuable.*

• *"The mind, as well as metals and elements, can be transmuted from degree to degree, from condition, from pole to pole, from vibration to vibration."*

• *"The rhythm can be neutralized by the art of polarization".*

• *"Nothing escapes from the principle of cause and effect, but there are many planes of Causation and one can use the laws of the superior plane to dominate those of the inferior one".*

• *"The wise person serves in the superior, but it governs in the inferior. It obeys the laws that are above it, but in its own plane and in those that are below it, it governs and orders. However. In doing so, it is part of the principle rather than oppose it.*

*The wise person submerges in the Law, and by understanding its movements, operates in it instead of being his blind slave. Similarly to the good swimmer, he goes from here to there, according to his own will, instead of being dragged like the wood that floats in the current. Nevertheless, the swimmer, the wise person and the ignorant, are all submitted to the law. One who understands this goes in the good way that leads to the Adeptship."*

• *"The wise person to measurements, recognizing the relative unreality of the universe, imagines that he can defy its laws. That is nothing more than a silly and presumptuous, which will crash against the rocks and will be squashed by the elements, because of his madness".*

• *Everything is mind, the universe is mental The Kybalion.*

With this section... we conclude a small view of the content of the hermetic philosophy with regard to Satanism.

Without any doubt, who deepens in these principles, understand them, apply them and learn to use them in their daily life, in the mental and material planes, you will realize that they dominate the world.

Somehow extraordinary what is expressed here is something that you already knew and remembered, power is latent in everyone.

# PAZUZU

# ORIGINAL SATANISM

To open a so complex door like Satanism is, it is not an easy mental adventure to assimilate and even less, when it is the end of god.

Due to this concept, it is required that whoever reads the following sections, forget to "believe" by faith, and know, do not accept what is stated here, but analyze and think.

Before entering and crossing this infernal threshold, a reflection would be prudent.

Why or what is the reason for you to believe in god?

What really god has done for you, god, not you or other people?

Where did you get the knowledge about god, did you investigate it or did they impose on you?

How many gods are there?

All your knowledge about god is based only on what the Bible says, and what was imposed to you from childhood, Easter movies, Christmas, mass every eight days, baptism, confirmation, etc., all that drama with which your mind was permeated so deeply that you "firmly believe" that god exists.

And on the same line simultaneously they imposed to you the devil as the staunch enemy of god.

Thus in your great ignorance of believing, you succumbed in total submission and you spurned the other, neither of them ever existed.

But well, this is the same, a text that says that what you believe is not true, is a bold statement; but what bases are there to say it ...? Let's look without imposing a concept or a truth or anything less, just a little history before entering into the same hell. Nobody really knows when the Sumerian people existed, the Anunnaki or skywalkers, and less when the hyperboreans inhabited the Earth.

I will not deep into the history of these peoples, but we go directly with the theme ...

It doesn't exist record about the appearance date of these civilizations, the first culture and the first writing of humanity neither of god nor angels nor demons, nor humans who wrote.

After all this, the Sumerians told a series of stories, myths, legends of gods and enchanted beings, a countless events and technologies that were discovered in our time.

This people disappear without a reason, but there are their memories, clay tablets with all their knowledge.

A strange language, as well as strange stories about very special beings, extraordinary artifacts whose graphic and physical representations ... amaze anyone.

Constructions, flying machines, watches, construction machinery, philosophical knowledge, stellar knowledge, solar computers, nuclear energy, mysterious beings of darkness, spirits, entities of the night....

All that ... more than 15,000 years ago ... and maybe much more time in the past.

Let's look at some images that still exist of this incredible civilization.

Nobody can imagine something that has not seen, the tablets with the first language of humanity, speak about

other histories and others gods, about places lost in space and time, about incredible events, which for that nascent humanity were totally improbable.

Think about how life was on the planet 15,000 years ago, where they got all the information, who was their teacher, how they built the man barely lived in huts.

When modern man discovered these texts, they were already ruins.

In the Middle East the independence of a nation without a homeland was born in the third century B.C. King Plolomeo II, rescued Sumerian histories, he created the 70 wise persons or exegetes that translated and distorted history, creating the bible. And ... thereafter the business of god.

Everything began with the "Epic of Gilgamesh", the rest is history.

God's version was complete but that of the devil was hidden, the fantastic powers of a type of identity with extraordinary knowledge about occult sciences were only revealed to few ones and now to you. SATANISM ....

# Ningishzida

[Sumerian deity Ningishzida accompanied by two griffons. It is the oldest image of snakes that is known 8000 b.C.]

The beginning of the caduceus of wisdom, the beginning of magic and the power of nature.

# PAZUZU

"I am Pazuzu, son of Anu, King of the demons of the air who descend
with force from the mountains, making havocs"

# LAMASHTU

**Lamashtu**, the lady of hell and mother of all demons. If the devil and god had existed, she would be the one who gave birth to them.

Although looking in another context is the mother of gods and demons.

The church founded its creed on combating it, knew the texts written on the Sumerian tags and found in them the essence of sacred power, the wisdom to act, the rituals of nature, the infinite power of blood and menstruation, magic of the perfect number 6.

A mental and natural power of such force that it should be totally hidden to the profane, the power of magic, and nothing better than creating in its environment, a halo of misfortunes, despair, misery, disgust, contempt, degradation, and to impose those concepts with death.

Like this was born the devil, hell, hate towards the women, the machismo, the contempt for blood, the maddening fear to the **666**.

And for 2.000 years the world believed and it continues believing.

**Lamashtu,** Pazuzu's wife, basically the church turned her into the mother of all human aberrations, devouring of fetuses, bloodied uteruses, begot the hellish demons, it killed children to devour them, nothing could be further from reality... from this legend, born countless supposed rituals of mental disorders, cannibalism, murders, rapes, sacrifices, all attributed to the demon father of darkness.

**Lamashtu**, she was the adored daughter of An, and his wife Ki, the creative gods of the Sumerian culture and of all that exists.

As everything related to the church lies and deceptions, it was responsible for distorting the knowledge of power, the same that transcended through other cultures. The same meaning with different goddesses and gods ...

It is undoubtedly the creation of hell and the devil along with Ningishzida, god that represents the beginning of creation, the essence of Eden, known in the Sumerian culture as "The lord of the tree of life", the story of genesis and biblical creation, is a gross copy of this god or goddess, taking into account that he is male woman, an androgynous, and without a doubt, the origin of the famous reptilians.

*In the roots of the past is the origin of the occult sciences, caught in them the birth of gods and demons.*

# RITUALS

## *"Wicca, Rituales Secretos de Magia y Brujería" (Book) [Wicca, Secrets Rituals of Magic and Witchcraft]*

The same elements used in witchcraft rituals, are the same used with Satanism.

The difference is that the rituals of magic and witchcraft do not have in themselves the philosophy of the Satanist, in the great majority of occasions witches, magicians, sorcerers, they serve to Satanism.

Similarly, invocations, pacts, prayers and the dates of the Sabbat, magic symbols, spells, incantations, the whole issue about magic and witchcraft, is found in the different specific books to each topic.

There exists a series of beliefs that the rituals of Satanism require; a big five-pointed star, black and red candles, a naked woman placed on it, a merciless orgy of uncontrolled sex, and the famous black Christian curtains.

An inverted crucifix, there is no major stupidity in the Satanists than ignorance, Jesus never existed, there is no cross, there is nothing. But having it reversed is to accept its presence.

Or get a goat to slaughter it and like hungry hyenas drink its blood, or a child, or a woman, or a man, or to kill six black cats thrown alive into boiling water, those are the concepts of the Church that hides its perversities and aberrations created by its god.

Today some are called satanics and satanists, dressed in black full of piercings, extravagant tattoos, and black lipstick, that is nothing more than ridiculing a deep philosophy in the hands of the misfits. Equal they are free... but far from Satanism.

A theater a little dramatic, rude copy of the tabernacle, today represented in churches, temples, etc.

In the roots of the past there is the origin of the occult sciences, caught in them the birth of gods and demons.

## *Exodus 40 - Queen Valera Antigua 1602*
### "Moses erects the Tabernacle

1. AND JEHOVAH spoke to Moses, saying:

2. On the first day of the first month, you'll raise the Tabernacle, the Tabernacle of witness:

3. And yo shall put in it the ark of the testimony, and you shall enclose it with the veil:

4. And you shall put the table in order: you shall also put the candlestick and you shall light its lamps:

5. And you shall put the altar of gold for the perfume before the ark of the testimony, and you shall put the pavilion before the door of the tabernacle.

6. Then you shall put the altar of the holocaust in front of the door of the tabernacle, of the tabernacle of the testimony.

7. Then you shall place the source between the tabernacle of the testimony and the altar; and you shall put water in it.

8. Finally, you shall place the atrium around it, and the Pavilion of the Atrium door.

9. And you shall take the anointing oil and you shall anoint the tabernacle and all that is in it; and you shall sanctify it with all its glasses, and it shall be holy.

10. And you shall anoint the altar of holocaust and all its glasses: and you shall sanctify the altar, and it shall be a most holy altar.

11. Also you shall anoint the source and its base, and you shall sanctify it.

12. And you shall bring Aaron and his sons to the door of the tabernacle of the testimony, and you shall wash them with water.

13 And you'll dress Aaron the Holy garments, and you shall anoint him, and you shall consecrate him so that he will be my priest.

14. Then you'll bring his children, and you'll dress them with tunics:

15. And you shall anoint them as you anointed their father, and they will be my priests: and it will be that their anointing will serve them by perpetual priesthood throughout their generations.

16. And Moses did agreeing all that Jehovah commanded him; this way he did it."


From there the altar of the god and devil, the same thing with different end, for god a grill, for some the place of rituals. Hence was born the great richness and wealth of the temples of the church.


"Leviticus 5 - Reina Valera Antigua 1602


1. AND WHEN a person would sin, that would hear the voice of who swore, and he would be witness who saw, or knew, if he didn't denounce it, he will take his sin.

2. Likewise the person who has touched anything filthy, either dead body of filthy beast, or dead body of filthy animal, or dead body of filthy reptile, if he didn't not know it, he will be filthy and he will have committed a crime:

3. Or if he would touch a filthy man in any of his filth of which he is unclean, and he'll not let him see; if he later gets to know it, he will be guilty.

4. Also the person who will swear, pronouncing with his lips do evil or good, in whatever things the man utters with an oath, and he does not know it; If he later understands it, he will be blamed in one of these things.

5. And when he would sin in any of these things, he will confess what he sinned.

6. And for his expiation he will bring to Jehovah for his sin that he has committed, a female of the herds, a lamb or a goat as an offering of atonement; and the priest shall make atonement for him of his sin.

7. And if it would be not enough for a lamb, he shall bring in atonement for his sin which he committed, two turtledoves or two young pigeons to Jehovah; one for expiation, and other for holocaust.

8. And he shall bring them to the priest, who shall offer the one that is is for expiation, and he shall separate its head from its neck, without separate it completely:

9. And he shall sprinkle the blood of the expiation on the wall of the altar; and what remains of the blood he will squeeze it at the foot of the altar; it is expiation.

10. And with the other one he will do the holocaust according to the rite; and he'll di for him, the priest the expiation of the sin he committed, and he will be forgiven.

13. And the priest will make expiation for him for his sin that he committed in any of these things, and he will be forgiven; and the excess will be of the priest, as the present of food. Expiatory offerings

14. Jehovah spoke more to Moses, saying:

15. When someone will commit fault and sin by weapons in the things sanctified to Jehovah, he'll bring his expiación to Jehovah, mutton without blemish from the herds, according to his estimation, in silver shekels of the sanctum shekel, in gift for the sin:

16. And he'll pay that one of the holy things in which he will have sinned, and he'll add to it the fifth one, and he will give it to the priest: and the priest will do expiation for him with the mutton of the sacrifice for the sin, and he will be forgiven.

17. Finally, if a person will sin, or he will do some of all those things that for order of Jehovah will not be done, even without doing it knowingly, he is guilty, and he will take his sin.

18. So he'll bring the priest for expiation, according to his estimation, mutton without blemish from the herds: and the priest will do expiation for him for his weapon that committed by ignorance, and he will be forgiven.

19. It is infraction, and truly he committed an offense against Jehovah."

A business of the expiation of sin, what many don't know is that god only eats meat, and he likes the sacrifices.

## Excerpt from the book Viaje a Apocalipsis *[Travels to the Apocalypse]*

## OFFERINGS

Let's see what were the tributes that liked to Jehovah, to start no vegetables, a circumstance that poor Cain ignored, who in his ingenuousness dared to bring the best of his fruits and logical came the rejection and acceptance of the fat sheep that Abel carried, and if you do not believe me, let's look at what Jehovah says to him when asking how the offerings should be consecrated:

(Leviticus 3:3 to 5)

"Then he shall offer the sacrifice of peace, as an offering lit to Jehovah, the fat that covers the intestines, and all the fat that is on the entrails, and the two kidneys and the fat that is on them, and on the loins; and with the kidneys he'll remove the fat from the intestines that is on the liver. And the sons of Aaron shall burn it on the altar, on the holocaust that shall be on the wood that shall be on the fire; it is a offering of pleasant smell for Jehovah".

This seems more a roast than a consecration and if we put it in doubt, the "Lit offering" I think is nothing more than meat roasting.

(Exodus 29 13 and 14)

"You shall also take all the fat that covers the intestines, the fat above the liver, the two kidneys, and the fat that is above them, and you shall burn it on the altar. But the meat of the calf, and its skin, and its dung, you shall burn them with fire outside the camp; it is an offering for sin."

The above mentioned, is or not roasted!

He did not like the leftovers, only the most tender meat (by the way, if you want to see a similar barbecue, I invite you to have a tour around the outskirts of Bogota next weekend along the northern highway near the towns of Chía, Cajicá, (Colombia), there they sell a delicious roasts accompanied by guacamole that I swear that Jehovah had would tasted them to the fullest except that he did not like vegetables).

And the barbecue is prepared!

(Exodus 29:17 and 18)

"You shall cut the mutton into pieces, and you'll wash its intestines and its legs, and you'll put them on its pieces and on its head. And you shall burn the whole mutton on the altar; holocaust of pleasant smell for Jehovah".

Wow, wow, or better oh! Oh, pleasant smell for Jehovah, delicious! And what better than to accompany it with bread, cakes, puff pastries, etc. Only missed the beer. And to continue the celebration:

(Exodus 29:22 to 25)
"Then you shall take from the mutton the fat, and the tail, and the fat that covers the intestines, and the fat of the liver, and the two kidneys, and the fat that is on them, and the right shoulder; because he is mutton of consecration. Also a big cake of bread, and a cake of bread of oil, and a puff-pastry of the basket of unleavened bread presented to Jehovah, and you'll put everything in the hands of Aaron and in the hands of his children; and you will deserve it as a wave offering before the Jehovah. Then you shall take him from his hands and you shall burn it on the altar, on the holocaust, for pleasant smell in front of Jehovah. It is a lit offering to Jehovah".

That odor should give an appetite, exquisite! Imagine for a moment the priests and the poor Aaron rocking all the meat and passing saliva, this is a great cruelty, but in some ways he was kind, let's look what he leaves:

(Exodus 29:26)
"And you shall take the breast of the mutton of the consecrations, which is of Aaron, and you shall rock it for a wave offering before the Jehovah; and it shall be your portion."

That is the law of the funnel they are single bones or ribs. Ah! But there was a drink, although not exactly beer.

(Exodus 29:40)
"In addition, with each lamb a tenth part of an ephah of flower flour mixed with the fourth part of an hin of crushed olive oil; and for the libation, the fourth part of a hin of wine".

In this way it was the consecration and if the one who approached was not a priest, it would easily die!

(Numbers 3:10)
"And you shall constitute to Aaron and his sons so that they may exercise their priesthood; and the stranger who will approach, he will die."

I think there was something very strange there, would be that Jehovah needed to feed a large group of people? And what better way than to build a steakhouse, servants, pardon, some priests and a naive people who would provide them food or otherwise what did he do with so much meat? We'll see. But it happens that there were certain clarifications or pleasures to take into account, apparently they could not eat, or maybe that they would gain weight? And since sugar was not known honey was rejected.

(Leviticus 11-2)

"Any offering that you would offer to Jehovah will be with leavening; because from no leaven, nor any honey, shall be burned any offering for Jehovah.-

## MENUS FOR JEHOVAH

Just for information, let's see the offerings or the menu that was ordered according to the case:

## ROASTED AND BAKED FOODS

(Leviticus 2:4)

"When you offer an offering baked in the oven, it shall be of unleavened flour cakes mingled with oil, and unleavened puff pastry spread with oil".

## FRIED FOODS

(Leviticus 2 5)

"But if you offer a skilful offering in pan, it shall be of flower flour without yeast, mixed with oil."

## COOKED FOODS

(Leviticus 2:6 and 7)

"Which you shall divide into pieces, and you shall pour oil upon it; it is offering. If you offer an offering cooked in a pot, it shall be made of flower flour with oil."

It seems that the function of the priests was to be more chefs than evolved spirituals and they had the responsibility of a good seasoning for "pleasant smell to Jehovah."

(Leviticus 2:9)
"He shall take out the memorial portion from the grain offering and burn it on the altar as a food offering, an aroma pleasing to Jehovah".

In addition, it had to be seasoned very well.

(Leviticus 2:13)
"And you shall season all your grain offerings with salt. Do not leave the salt of the covenant of your god out of your grain offerings; you shall add salt to all your offerings".

But no vegetables. Now I understand why he despised Cain, the poor man had no idea that the vegetables did not go with the Jehovah's diet. Let's see now how to keep the full provisions or the so-called offerings for "peace" (what particular tastes).

So religion and many groups of Satanism took the same course, emulating all this, creating similar rituals, close to the aberrant.

It is not difficult to find everywhere **TEMPLES OF SATAN**, the church of satan, satanism, satanic temple, office of divination where are sold and offered pacts with demons.

A similar theatre with the church of god, benches, rugs, Atrium, facing an inverted crucifix, on the other side the image of Baphomet, a gigantic five-pointed star, all hooded, black candles, blood of goat, at the entrance the 666, a nude female ready and prepared for all kinds of humiliations, a total circus of perversion.

That is far, far away from the true Satanism. It is nothing more than the same business of belief, the antithesis of god is not a place, it is a mental state, one is limitation and submission, and the other is freedom.

How little power has, one that required blood of a living being, when he could get it from itself, according to the bible god needs that sinners offer him flesh and blood expiate their sins, which small and miserable business of the faith. True rituals of Satanism are not the antithesis of religion; the true altar is in nature and its elements or the old religion or witchcraft.

# Guilt and self-pity

When beginning the performance of the rituals, the struggle between what is imposed as sin and the freedom that is required stands out in the mind.

It has been lived trapped in the submission of the mind, on its knees, in the worst unworthy submission of the human being is proclaimed the "sinful self", the total self-condemnation. (Of course they knew it by memory, it is not necessary to transcribe it)

This mental technique, nullifies, severs, castrates freedom, and is the brake of who fights that strives to break the ties of the thought.

The fear, the terror, the thought that prosecutes the act proclaims it from the punishment of god, it makes that the Satanist doubts, he questions that he is not free, that he is a slave of the dogma, that he lacks to his church, that his life will be a misfortune.

Self-pity and guilt destroy him, it is something that everyone must fight at the bottom of his being, you are in this world to live, to serve yourself, to enjoy life in all its representations, to give yourself what you want, without limits.

***The real sin lies in doing not what you want***, the constant abstention and the denial of temptation.

Satan lavishes the total temptation, indeed he imposes it as a preamble to power, no one who does not accept or is tempted to change, will change, no one who is not valued, will be valued, no human being who does not seek to be tempted to succeed, will triumph.

And those who do not feel tempted, are miserable, unhappy who try to atone for their desires by paying and submitting their minds to the vile executioners messengers of a god of lies, who will continue to oppress the pocket of the

unfortunate, who destroys his life for forgiving the sin of feeling.

Who does prevent you to be a millionaire? God

Who does condemn you and submit you to humiliation? God

Who does blame you for your natural desires for pleasure that produces free sex? God

Who does judge even in the depths of your privacy? God

Who does welcome for being a miserable bastard, that in your renounce to live? God

The list is endless ... everything is prohibited, do not look, do not touch, do not think, do not try, do not do, do not go, do not feel...

But strangely, what is most condemned and forbidden is what is most yearns, sex with the forbidden couple, wealth, fortune, beauty, freedom, another infinite list of unsatisfied desires that, by not supplying them, carrying to the misfortune of the soul.

The Church skillfully, from childhood has created ment all barriers with a forced but well-organized story, sins with which the soul is lost.

## GREED

The lustfulness is the bastion of the essence of the Satanism where all philosophy take shape, nobody neither in his world, nor in other worlds, not in any world, can achieve something that does not covet.

The foundation stone of power is the greed of wisdom, of property, of material goods, of the pleasures that enhance the soul, of well being, to covet is to be more, stopping being less.

Coveting is the greatness of the life; it is the engine that impels to fight, to reach every time more, the greed must be the daily motivation of the life.

You are a greedy born, you just do not know it yet, and you are the most greedy of your world, you won 2,500,000 of spermatozoids to be here reading these lines.

Only a greedy can achieve such a feat ... you must check if that greed disappeared by submission to others.

# ENVY

It goes hand in hand with greed, you only covet what somehow you envy, envy is the mother of growth, of improvement, of progress, of gain, of love, of war, is the mother of ALL THE PROGRESSES...

Envy leads to competition, to the challenge of being better, to the challenge of winning; the best way to overcome the limitation is to envy those who have already done it.

When seeing the car of the neighbor, the thought of envy startles, well for him who got it, but I want a better one, the competition has begun.

Those who travel are the best sellers of travel for those around them.

The woman who gets ready, she takes care of her, she is beautiful, she is the best seller of beauty.

The envy has the strongest magnetic power that exists, there is a reason, in your genetics you are competitive, you do not like to be left behind, you do not like to be less, you do not like to be one more, you want to be always the best before others, but you refuses to do so.

The god of lies is the largest envious, an unhappy that prefers to see his creation in misery that in greatness, that's what sells the religion, to be miserable.

In all the bible you will never find a word of motivation to reach your achievements... well you have to pray to god... and pay him.

The real envy only the winners have, the losers race of the unhappy feel guilty of feeling, they perish in their mental conformism empty of illusions.

When they feel envy, they go to confess them, they beat their breast, they pray a hundred I sinful, they do penance, and they carry the savings to pay ... that is why they go to the sky of the miserable, not to the hell of the winners.

# PRIDE

Would not be proud whom that, by greed and envy, has triumphed over others? Pride is the recognition of achievement, it is the prize of the winner, the greatest stimulation of the ego, pride is the freedom to excel where others failed.

The truth of the condemnation of pride is to prevent that others from greed and envy, achieve goals, reach challenges and defies, be great and reach far away from the dogma limiting submission. Every conquest, every achievement, every feat, every act of complacency, is a product of pride, and whoever achieves it has the obligation to feel proud of himself, all achievement of others, should be a pride for the family, should stimulate envy and greed in others, so that they also achieve it.

Those who do not feel pride, is because they have never done anything worthwhile, and if they do something they owe it to god.

Nobody achieves anything without effort, discipline, perseverance, persistence, rigorousness, dedication, and that constant effort gives pride, and whoever does

278

it, once, will always do more ... the Satanist does not conform with small achievements...

## LUST

Does not deserve a big award the one that has achieved to conquer a big goal?, It should be condemned to who has reached the top of success?, Do you know what lust means? Quickly exceeded sex... that's what the priests say.

No, lust means "abundance of what you need", it comes from the latin Luxus, luxury, now well, what does it need?

Exactly, what makes the church full of luxuries and extravagance, sex, gold, riches that show in front of the poor ones, but they condemn in others what they do, turning it into sin, and who believes them, he accepts with resignation his misery.

Lust is the prize of being the best, the sum of greed, envy, the corresponding with pride, a great fighter will not live in misery, will live as he wishes with the best.

Lust is free, in all that represents, the limit does not exist, a cent a billion, a woman a harem, a man or a hundred. Who came up with a man for a woman, or a woman for a man?

The freedom of everyone is his freedom, how much does he want and what?

To be lustful is not only to desire it, it is to create it, nobody can have lust for a desire, lust is what you get after fighting, not before doing it.

The rest have what you want and can keep, it is worthless to have much and bad. But if you can have a lot and good, you will awaken envy for others to follow you, feel proud and worthy of your achievements.

Lust is the total virtue that moves to the world to live in welfare and equity, without lust just the worst of miseries of the soul would remain.

## GLUTTONY

Again, you know its real meaning, not the one they have sold you, the real one.

Gluttony means throat, swallow, in other words, know how to eat.

Like everything, god does not allow, he flatly forbids to eat well.

Who does not like to eat well, satiate the appetite, the story that is eating too much does not work, if you are satisfied you are harassed, no matter how much you want to eat and eat you cannot, gluttony does not exist, but there is an eating disorder.

Many of the church are obese; of course, they eat a lot and don't do anything, just like the pigs in the pigsty only to fatten. At the time of the Inquisition, they charged for everything and one of the requirements was the large banquets that were to be given ...

Eating is a pleasure, an enjoyment, a right, to eat well, you have to work, to demand you must covet, envy, fight and be tempted to conquer your challenges, in doing so the pride of achieving it deserves the prize of lust and in the lust the good eating.

But hungry people do not think, they are weak, they do not fight, they are easier to control, hunger leads to misery, to conformism to the denial of being.

Gluttony is eating well, but it is a sin, die of hunger and serve god ... Satan says eat until you are satisfied ... and enjoy the pleasure of the food you have obtained...

God says: with the sweat of your forehead you will eat your bread, but if you eat more you commit the sin of gluttony and you will be condemned.

## LAZINESS

Nothing better on a Sunday afternoon, after a week of work, a good lunch, a good sex and an afternoon of laziness.

For the god's foremen, the rest must not exist, without pleasures and without rest, the wretches do not think, work hard all week and on Sunday go to be emptied, and leave the laziness go three times to mass. The rest is deserved, on you and nobody else depends the quantity of it, on you and nobody else depends the demand of the task that must be fulfilled.

Never allow your well-deserved rest to be interrupted, because someone else wants to impose it, to avoid that, fight for your life with all the possible desire ...

## ANGER

Anger is the primary defense of all beings before the attack, he is condemned to limit that precisely defend himself, fight to not accept what is imposed, and obviously stop the flow of courage when the deception is discovered.

Anger is condemned, so that submission prevails, so that the right of defense is buried, entering into total acceptance.

(Matthew 5:38-48)
"You have heard that it was said, 'Eye for eye, and tooth for tooth. But I tell you, do not resist an evil person. If anyone slaps you on the right cheek, turn to him or her other cheek also. And if anyone wants to sue you and take your tunic, hand over also your coat; if anyone forces you to go one mile, go with them two miles.

Give to the one who asks you, and do not turn away from the one who wants to borrow from you. You have heard that it was said: Love your neighbor and hate your enemy.

But I tell you, love your enemies and bless those who curse you, do good to those who hate you, and pray for those who spitefully use you and persecute you; that you may be children of your Father in heaven, it causes his sun to rise on the evil and the good, and sends rain on the righteous and the unrighteous".

The worst of the worst, the maximum insolence to submission and the maximum preparation to avoid the uncontrolled rabble before the deception. Who can love the evil that causes damage, the thief, the rapist, if you get a hit, return five.

What better than an idiot and slavish that it does not have a load, but two, love your enemies, perhaps it not reward them and put your head under his feet.

This has a strong mental content, a brake to the reaction, a prevention before the awakening of consciences, today is seen in the trials, in the gaps of human law that reward criminals, who will undoubtedly continue to commit crimes. Rewarding the crime with the assumption of stopping it, is nothing more than strengthening sending the message of reward to new offenders.

The anger is the force of Justice, to combat an evil, is only possible with a greater evil, although the intention that moves it is different.

Without anger there is no dignity, anger is justice that maintains balance in coexistence, to the good, noble and idiot, always going wrong, for who is respected everything works.

Thus, the Satanist, must understand the deep essence of the freedom of being, away from dogma, guilt, sin and submission, otherwise, you cannot apply this infinite knowledge of freedom.

# THE SUPREME RITUAL
# THE STRATEGY

A Satanist is a shadow, he hides in the shadows, he does not rise up, he is discreet, he avoids salutations, he does not accept the protocols, he lives in his inner world creating, conquering, achieving his goals, creating his world and being unique, not contaminated with suffering and unhappiness of others, he deeply understands that it is the freedom of each one.

**A Satanist is a strategist.**
To use the least resource to get the most profit, fight and succeed without fighting, achieve achievements with the least effort.

In magic (witchcraft) like in Satanism, polarities do not exist, as we saw in Hermetic principles.

There is no good or evil, only freedom, no black or white magic, only intention; everything has a gentle rhythm between two poles.

Good and evil, are only concepts according to the rewards, if you win is good, if you lose is bad.

In Satanism there is no good or evil, there is only the strategy, the total power to do, the Satanist creates his world, looks at goals, projects, knows and recognizes that only he will shape his world, he becomes predator, seeks options, breaks boundaries, acts in the shadows, knows the strategy of winning, understands that the law of compensation acts in all nature, therefore, will not give anything without having nothing.

He will always think about how to give less and to have more, do not interpret this comment as an apology to abuse, Satanism tends to intelligence in the wise use of options.

The best lawyer is who knows the gaps of the laws and with that he triumphs, but to know the gap he must know and recognize all laws.

The satanist woman, endowed by nature, uses her manipulation in her favor not against her, and triumphs.

Since there is no good or bad, there is no condemnation, no one can do it, even the millionaire with ill-gotten money buys the conscience of the judge, the poor and miserable, although innocent, is always condemned.

Now perhaps you understand where the phrase "The scapegoat" was born, its origin in goats, to pay for sins. What is the guilt of the goat sacrificed bestially before the tabernacle of God, of the carnal desires inhibited and condemned by the same god?

All Satanist group must create its own conditions of action, business, exchange, projects, the group must grow like a group and in turn individually in each of the tasks performed in its daily lives.

The primary group will be kept away from the sub-groups that are created, such as conferences, lectures, cults, revelations and rituals.

Church is equal, they have an accumulation of secondary businesses, the difference is that they monopolized everything, therefore, that will be its misfortune.

On the contrary, Satanism generates growth for everybody, everybody give, all win, just like in nature the hierarchy of growth is required, the lion does not hunt, the females do it, but it is the first that will eat, but … he will also be the first to face danger and protect them.

There is no slavery in Satanism, all are free to growth, but a true Satanist does not waste a chance to win.

The bear, in autumn, does not skimp on food, it needs fat for the winter, it does not waste anything. That strategy makes him survive, the coyote, demanding in his food, dies of hunger.

Never the Satanist will obtain nothing with the suffering of another, he will not contaminate himself of unnecessary pain, for that he knows the laws, nobody will plow in the desert.

The Satanist will not participate or make pacts or treaties with anyone. He always looks for what he can give, what contribute him to get more power.

In this section is where the decision must be made, a woman who lives with a man who does not fight, a conformist, a scrounger, but she feels that she can grow and reach other goals, she will have to allow the anger of disenchantment acts, to make decisions, to migrate, to leave, to change, to give her other opportunities, to seek and to use the options in her favor and based on the strategy triumphs.

But if her mind is anchored in a conservative thought limited by dogma, she will accept her misery without doing anything.

The strategy takes power to the maximum point, a witch knows the secrets of being, she lives in the light and in the darkness, she takes the opportunity, she is discreet, doesn't mind the man married, unmarried, she gets power in knowing the secrets, she exceeds the limit, only she knows that and triumphs.

A good magician can rule an empire, without sitting on the throne, that is for the superb king who does not know who commands.

A man has ten lovers, a woman has ten lovers, and nobody knows them.
A man has business nobody knows.
Shadows among the shadows fight without fighting, be without being, see without being seen.

The art of manipulation is the art of the silent strategist, why they are not so easily found or made known, or: Are you of those who believe that people choose their rulers? Those who rule and dominate are Satanists shadows.

How many men and women do believe firmly that they are in charge in home? Maybe the lover is in charge.

There are few who suspect that there are invisible threads that move on their head moved by hands they do not imagine, what would you like to be, the puppet or the puppeteer? See the book *"Arte de la Estrategia y Manipulación Mágica" [Art of Strategy and Magic Manipulation]*

Every satanist group is a hidden group, far from the common, great businessmen, great manipulators, big businessmen who use the weaknesses of others to gain, the same natural principle of triumph.

Today, there are a countless number of ancient sects descended from the last Templars, sects and groups hidden away from the common people; they are the ones who govern the world.

# SEX BLOOD AND SATANISM

A complex but attractive theme, Satanism has almost always been linked to blood and sex.

Somehow or another, the mind generates through information, to receive a myriad number of stereotypes that constitute the Satanist world.

It is worth clarifying two issues: one thing is to be Satanist and another satanic.

Satanists are tose that profess the philosophy of Satanism, symbols, knowledge, masses, freedom, mental anarchy, etc.

Satanists, groups difficult to define, combine religions, mix rituals, execute aberrant acts, do not possess philosophical direction, imitate epochs, with abrupt personality changes, where sexual abuse is one of their expressions.

To enter with this theme you must have an open mind away from concepts imposed or beliefs rooted on sexual behaviors. Satanism has a great sexual content, this obeys with the same principle of generation, the most important instinct of every species, is the survival instinct.

Survival is produced by sexual function, specifically without sex there is no species.

Sexuality has been tarnished by a myriad of concepts, none has the truth and less this writing.

Based solely on the natural concept, sexuality is applied in this way in Satanism, within the maximum purity that the wisdom of nature shows us.

The essence of life or survival instinct goes hand in hand with the basic essence of life support, blood.

Without sex there are no species, without blood there is no life. Based on the above, let's look at the topic.

## SEX

Like in other philosophies, in Satanism the sexual gender man or woman does not exist.

The creative principle is woman-man, there could not exist one or the other, or both at the same time. This brings us to the concept of the androgynous, the descendents of the creation, have simultaneously both sex genders.

295

A lunar and hormonal variation stimulates one gender over the other, female and male.

Basically the change is in the genitals, an external organ and an internal organ. For the rest ... physically and anatomically, in all species, the bodies are similar.

Now, in the case of humans, everything is exactly the same with some variations according to the physical constitution.

Internal organs have the same characteristics; liver of a man is similar to the one of a woman, the stomach of a woman similar to that of the man and as well with everyone else.

Even the case of the man-man, has nipples, tits, or mammary glands; he produces the same prolactin or breast milk.

In the remote possibility that a fetus will be implanted in the skin of a man, the blood supply, or irrigation, producing an extreme hormonal change, could perfectly sustain life.

Many cases of "parasitic twins" fetuses within the fetuses have occurred.

Beyond that, there is the parthenogenesis, let's say that the z plan of nature to sustain a species, the capacity of an ovule to self-fertilize. It occurs normally in some species of insects and amphibians.

So sexuality has countless infinite probabilities.

Satanism does not recognize sexual gender, neither man nor woman, nor heterosexual, nor homosexual, nor asexual, for philosophy there is bisexuality, without imposing the concept, with the freedom of each one to express or not his sexuality as he wishes, in deeper stays, satanism tends to pansexuality.

From this postulate onwards only the freedom of expression remains, there is no marriage, there is free union, there is no commitment, only delivery, there is no fidelity more than itself, sexuality, desire, pleasure, is exclusive to each individual and not of the couple.

No satanist, man or woman, is guardian of the genitals and pleasures of the other, that is the exclusive territory of each one, and it acts according to his wishes.

Every relationship in Satanism is based on the principle of equity, no one should be the slave of another's love.

Any sexual act by aberrant that may seem, but previously agreed by the parties cannot be judged.

Contrary to some Eastern beliefs where marriage or sex with infants is allowed, in Satanism it is forbidden, you can not get sexual pleasure from fear, rape, pain or suffering.

The total sexual surrender must be agreed among those who share it.

All the sexual arts, sado, masochism, fetishism, orgies, exchange, plus the infinite variation of possibilities, everything that leads to an integral pleasure, without imposing, without violating, without inflicting pain, without it can appear aberrant or dirty, is accepted.

In this scale of sexuality it is not possible to doubt about the fantastic energy that is liberated, the human psyche is predisposed to a series of sexual incentives very little experienced by the commmon, aromas, tastes, games, sensations, morbidnesss, mental images of prohibited sex, fetishism, voyeurism, with or without participation.

Mental voyeurism, the morbid narrative of sexual relations of the couple with other people.

Nothing that brings sexual pleasure, under freedom and without imposition is condemned, on the contrary, Satanism suggests the maximum sexual enjoyment, masturbation, sex, discovering new sensations, increases the power of the apprentice.

We live in a prudish society, in which it is questioned what is desired.

## BLOOD

Normally, it is thought about the blood as the crimson liquid that flows from the heart, the dramatic deep red.

But... the blood has many and varied representations, ovulatory flow, semen, saliva, sweat, in strict sense, the menses with the biggest content of power.

To understand the essence of life, blood, is sensed why today in some places transfusions of young people to adults are made, as a source of eternal youth and it has given result.

All religions, philosophies, creeds, cults, peoples, civilizations, etc., have workshipped and worship the blood.

Let's look at something interesting, Where does the blood is made? No, the heart transports and impels the blood; the blood is manufactured in the deepest part of the being, in the bone marrow or marrow, as it is normally known. Through the veins and nutrient arteries, the blood flows; an incredible journey of power, from the depths, then the heart drives it throughout the body.

Vampires or bloodsuckers, they feed of blood, human vampires too, but, in Satanism, blood represents the fifth element or the fundamental stone.

Undoubtedly, one must speak about the supposed sacrifices of blood, animals, humans, virgin women, etc., everything that has accompanied Satan since the beginning.

In Satanism the power of blood is recognized, without a doubt, but the energy of death is also recognized.

A blood vampire, "will not feed" of a shaken, scared, nervous human being, although it receives the blood, this is contaminated with the energy of the terror, therefore, and the vampire will be affected.

Satanism recognizes the principle, life-to-life, death-to-death. Great magic rituals, which

require blood, do not require the death of the donor, either human or animal.

Contrary to the bible that calls for blood baths, anointing the blood, etc., about this subject, the bible despises the menses; the satanists and vampires value it.

(Leviticus 12:1-5)
"Jehovah spoke to Moses, saying: Speak to the sons of Israel, and tell them: 'A woman who becomes pregnant and gives birth to a son will be unclean for seven days, just as she is unclean during her monthly period.

On the eighth day the boy is to be circumcised. Then the woman must wait thirty-three days to be purified from her bleeding; she must not touch anything sacred or go to the sanctuary until the days of her purification are over. If she gives birth to a daughter, for two weeks the woman will be unclean, as during her period, then she must wait sixty-six days to be purified from her bleeding".

It is still difficult to define why the god of the Bible abhors women. If a daughter is born, twice filthy.

No life shall be destroyed to perform a Satanism ritual, blood, may be used but not his life.

Virgin blood is the power freely and voluntarily given pre preparation of the woman whom she chooses as her partner, not by imposition or desire, just as the menstrual blood will have the same condition.

To delve into this theme, refer to the book *"Vampirismo Psíquico" [Psychic vampirism]*

For obvious reasons the satanist magical content of the rituals of life are not transmitted in its entirety, through the blood. As you advance in knowledge, somehow they will come into your life. Remembering the hermetic axiom.

*"The lips of wisdom remain closed, except for the ear capable of understanding.*

*Wherever the traces of the Master are, there the ears of the one who is ready to receive his teachings are wide-open. When the ear is able to hear, then the lips come to fill them with wisdom".*

# RITUAL OF SATANISM BLACK MOON

**Date:** moon nights, on the Sabbat of old religion

**Place:** coven, energetic sites, ruins, natural sanctuaries, housings, rooms prepared for that purpose, halls in universities, rooms in houses.

**Requirements:** nobody knows anyone, but others invite everyone.

**Purpose:** domain and power.

The whole strategy of Satanism is reduced to a single ritual known as the black moon.

It is the basic ritual of a Satanist group or individually of the initiator.

A little attention with this theme will help you understand how satanist philosophy works. Let me remind you that in Satanism there is no good or evil, or moral dogmas, or convictions, sins, the strategy exists. Everything begins with a single individual, SATANIST, who initially applies the laws in him.

*Before proceeding let's clarify something, if you are one of those who wait for everything you have heard, that Satanism is to find a magical scroll with text offering all the power without doing anything, so easy, where you sign and give your soul, when Mephistopheles the Messenger of Satan or any demon appears to give you what you want, and with that you already have money, wealth, women, luxuries and a life of pleasures, or a series of supernatural powers, similar with the genius of the Aladdin's lamp, let me tell you that it is not so.*

*That does not exist like that.*

*But... yes, there is a latent power within you, an extraodinary force greater of that of the messenger of the devil, a power superior to any genius of a lamp, the wise use of the laws that govern this universe, everything you have read in this treaty if you apply it, you dominate it, you use it, you will get what you want.*

A Satanist starts by it, is the maximum ritual, to demand him to change, to transform the life, is to have and apply the power of 666, six **"Decretos de Satán" [Decrees of Satan].**

# First infernal decree
# I RENOUNCE

*From now on, at this moment, I renounce the enslavement of my soul, to the submission of my thought, from now and forever appears in my being the new start.*

*No one, neither god nor demon, will give me what I deserve, only I ... I can know what I want and only I can satisfy my desires.*

*From today I renounce the low passions whims of emotions, I will respect the freedom of others, without harm me or holding grudges, I renounce live the life that others live, preys of their devotions.*

*I renounce the cry of pity, I renounce to the failure of the soul, I renounce support in my life all those who sink in their misfortune.*

*From today and forever, I renounce the wealth that brings poverty, I renounce love that brings disappointment, I renounce be a slave of the mundane pleasures, I renounce be possessed by all the sleeplessness, I renounce forever the limits of the extremes, from and forever I renounce to live dead.*

*I renounce the beliefs, I renounce the miserable gods that satisfy his ego, contemplating my agony with disdain.*

*I renounce the agony of having in my life what I do not deserve; I give up living a miserable due to the caprice and submission of others.*

*I renounce being servile, I renounce the ties of blood, I renounce to please others.*

*I renounce to hold in my mind my destruction in favor of others, I renounce to sleep with sufferings for the actions of others, I give up abandoning my struggle for the welfare of others, I renounce god forever.*

# Second infernal decree
# Today I will be God and Demon

*I am the total creator of my life, I am the source of life and power incarnated in this body, I am the one who gives direction and power to my destiny, my actions move the environment of my life, I am a creator towards power, I am who dominates and not the dominated, I am the one who demands in the constant reason to live.*

*Nobody will create my dreams, or will supply my needs, I will not accept charity from others who in their charity will grant me, I will be the creator of my riches and poverty, I will be the creator of my joys and misfortunes, I will be the total creator of my destiny, without guilt or condemnations.*

*I am the creator, I possess the sacred power of nature, and with it I will transform my existence into the unique top of my desired world.*

*It is me who creates the cycles of change in my life, I am the controller of the ebb and flow of my passions, I am who guides this sacred body in the constant evolution of the beloved dreams.*

*I am god, without limits, I am demon, without limits, from today I will be like the hellish mirror, where I will give back three times, three times what they give me ... my power and my pride will be such, that so great is my love for good, as major it is my love for evil.*

*My power will be so strong that the same heaven and hell will disappear.*

*From today and forever, it will be my conviction, to dominate my world, without any passion, I will love the triple who loves me, and three times three I will despise the one who harms me.*

*From today I extract from my sacred essence the power that dominate*

*s the world in the dawn, from today and forever, I am god and devil in my mind.*

# Third infernal decree
# Mephistopheles and Pazuzu

*Two servants I possess, two spirits of animation, two forces accompany me in all my action.*

*The one possesses the power to make me grow, the other possesses the power of everything what I want to obtain.*

*Mephisto, the wise assistant, who will come out of my hell, to fully demand me to complete my tasks, I will put my demand above all until my goal is over, from today I will not have compassion, I will not leave anything pending in a corner, to the maximum this decree I will fulfill even when everything seems not to go well.*

*I ask you oh winged being from the darkness, torment my mind if you see me failing, from the infernal abyss I invoke you to my life, push me when you see me wavering.*

*Demand me mercilessly, that every day ... I can demand a little more, until with pride and satisfaction see completed my work, finished my task, to start again.*

*Stimulates my senses, I ask you with devotion, remove fatigue, laziness and resignation, do not allow me to justify myself with the apology of denial, on the contrary, motivate me with the pleasures of the flesh, they will be refuge and strength of my decision.*

*From today I start the first and difficult task, to train this body up to achieve its surrender, daily exercise, rest, pleasure and fun, every morning in the infernal mirror I will see the change that this body will have, that is my first task of my new life in freedom.*

*In the constant discipline of sport, my mind and my determination will be trained, there are no apologies to fail, if I cannot train my body much less I can dominate a world.*

*Every month a little will be, but in a year, no one will recognize me, mind and body in harmony with your help oh Mephisto, everything will be achieved.*

## Pazuzu

*My bastion and protector, wise guide that you inhabit in the infernal shadows, hidden from the sparkling flames that show your terrible presence, in your eyes that reflect the incandescent red of the burning flames that shine without stopping, where you look without eyelids to protect you, red your eyes like black your fangs, with your sharp claws that stripped everything, moving your wings come to fly.*

*Show me your wisdom to act in the shadows, melt me in dreams, to be able to torment, teach me the old arts of infernal power, to possess in the distance the sleepy bodies, to satiate the lust of all the senses, that everything remains secret and is a simple dream upon waking. Give me your wisdom of the world to dominate, to take advantage of night and day, to be without god's medium the best rival.*

*Oh Pazuzu winged being of the infernal world, show me the power hidden in the darkness, give me the brightness of the flames that cover the infernal ceiling, give me the power of the dead of the life to dominate.*

*I invoked you to my life, reveals your wisdom, give me signals where I should walk. When I feel my course confused, when everything seems to be wrong, this your image, as you've revealed to others, with me you will also do, you will possess my mind with the sacred inspiration of the infernal book, where destinies are dominated for everything to change.*

*While I give you the pleasures of the flesh that you like so much without equal, drink the blood that flows from this enchanted whore, in the sacred menstruation of this ritual.*

*I am your ardent phallus, as trident that now seeks in pleasure, to charge the price of your wisdom that you deliver each time. Abandon your infernal abode, cross the wall, come to teach, I ask and I order it, you will never ever leave me.*

*Stimulate my senses, teach me to listen, to perceive in the distance everything that has to happen, the secrets reveal me to know how to act, to feel without feeling, to see without seeing, to be without being, to work prodigies with just thinking.*

*Now and forever, my teacher will be you.*

# Fourth infernal decree
# The chest of the hell

*Today and forever, whatever happens and in my life, whatever happens, no one ever will know.*

*Everything acted, everything conquered, everything achieved, everything that hurts, everything that, of happiness, everything enchanted by demons created, will be kept in the infernal trunk.*

*Nobody cares about my existence, more than me who am its creator, I will not talk to anyone about my victories nor I will promulgate my glories, as acts of value, I will not be cocky, superb or petulant, no one should care.*

*I will not reveal my acts no matter which they are, much less I will reveal my pain, if I show myself presumptuous, soon I will be the result of betrayal, if I show my sorrows, the weakness shown will be my downfall.*

*A single love I'll have, others hidden will be in the infernal trunk, hidden always they must be, only love will be for my life, for my existence and my realization.*

*The other loves are only moments of occasion, human love, love of pleasure, love to earthly belongings, they are mental anchors that only produce disappointment.*

*The loves of the world are passionate attachments to material things, or the presences of people, who like obstacles end up devouring the crumbs of my creation.*

*It does not matter at all, all equally pain or satisfaction, at the bottom of the infernal trunk, forever in the flames consumed will remain.*

*I will not make a party for what arrives, it will be a temporary, I will not suffer for what is left, and just something new will come.*

*My work cycle, has no beginning or end, everything is renewed whenever the trunk will give.*
*In good something ends, something begins again, in good something begins also begins its final.*

*Nothing new, never new can be left, at the beginning of its use it begins to wear away, no matter what it is, it is always the same, people or things will eventually change, everything is just temporary, I don't become attached to the banal, never I will stop anything and nothing will stop me, feelings, triumphs, sorrows, riches, treasures, fortunes and loves, everything will happen, I will enjoy to the fullest their presence while in my existence, but from today and forever, every day they will be in the infernal trunk, tomorrow after sunrise, everything in my life begins again, the past calcined forever is.*

# Fifth infernal decree
# Shades of the hell

The day has 24 hours of light and 24 hours of darkness, the nature is gently lulled among summers, autumns, winters and springs. The moon changes every day, it hides and appears, in a constant game of brightness and darkness.

Everything in life is dual, light and darkness, one does not know, and has no idea of what takes place in the other, ever the Sun will know the Panther hidden in the night, nor the moon will know the magical flight of the eagles.

*From today this Decree will live in my life, I'll have my light and my darkness, I will create my sky and my hell, my world of virtue and my world of lust.*

*I will wander in two worlds, the one will not know about the other, my discretion and my secrets will be so deep, that I will melt in light and darkness, nobody will know my arcane if it is not for my lips, and these, forever will be closed.*

• I will not lie, every lie hides a truth.

• I will not trick, I have the wisdom to obtain what I want without false promises.

• I will not accept commitments, I create my commitments, with my conditions.

• I will be mysterious, I dominate and rule my world.

• I will not promise anything to anyone or myself, I will create realities.

• Sincerity is my property, I will not tell my life, nor will publish my actions.

• I will have not friends, they hide in their presence the worst enemies.

• I will have not friends, they will always be rivals.

• Doors of my hell will be open to supporters who fight for my convictions, I will not fight for those of them.

• My life has a life that I must take care of, i will not take care of anyone's life, each one must watch over his life.

• I will be generous and kindly three times three, who deserves it.

• I will never expect payment or reward for my actions, I am my reward.

• I will give because I wish to give, I will not make of love a business.

• Whoever enters my darkness will know my conditions before entering; I will not force anyone to stay or to leave.

• I will value to the maximum those who are with me, I will be their full support

• I will ignore those who ignore me.

• I will not enter into the cause of others, I create my causes.

• I will not compete with others, I compete with myself.

• Whenever possible, and circumstances allows it, I wll give me the best of the best, I deserve it.

• I will avoid debts as much as possible, both in terms of money and labor, as well as moral debts.

• I will pay the fair and a little more.

• I will always be without being.

• Always before asking for help, I will look for solutions by my own means, I will have the pride of being, the help will be my last resort and it will be well rewarded for not having debts of gratitude.

• My pleasures are only mine, those who share them will be for their freedom not by imposition.

• My hell has only one lock, the one who enters has the key to enter, but when he leaves he loses it.

• I will not be contaminated with stories of pain and suffering of others, but I will be of help as soon as I could and is possible.

• I will not promote money to anyone, but I will encourage the progress of each one.

• My main value, dignity, I will not accept in my world people committed to family and children.

• I will never be a cause of pain in the lives of strangers, whoever cheats me will leave my life forever, if he returns he will only destroy me.

• I will enjoy the carnal pleasures, while the pleasure lasts, I will not create bonds of feelings with ties.

• From now forever I will work hard for my livelihood, I will be prudent in the use of material goods, I will always seek progress in study, work, advance and fortune.

• In my elderly only what I have sown counts.

• I will learn to be alone.

• My children are the children of the time, with their own hopes, dreams and desires, I will never impose mine on theirs, I will be their support, but not their provider.

• I will not be tied to a single person, nor I will not report back, nor I will submit to a whim, my dark side is only mine.

• I will promote to make happy those who deserve it.

• No one can ever deceive me, everyone deceives himself.

• I will never be custodian or guardian of another's genitals or their wishes, everyone is free.

• I will not have jails or prosecutors, I will avoid interrogating or condemning the freedom of others, I will also avoid knowing what does not matter to me.

• I cannot change the past, but I can modify my present and my future.

• I will not be contaminated with the past of others and less with mine.

• My amusements will be that, amusements not vices.

• I do not have anything, to not be possessed by anything.

# Sixth infernal decree
# Freedom

*The absolute reign of freedom will be my refuge. From today and forever, my life is my creation, no one else cares, to inhabit this body has been my choice from other lives, and it will be my choice for other lives.*

*Everything that happens in my existence is and will be because I have desired it, however, I will learn the lesson of the beings that rule and dominate the destiny, nothing happens for a reason but for the future mystery enclosed in for what.*

*Today I understand that this temporary experience of my spirit incorporated in this skin, has the power of total freedom, I am the one who wanders through the labyrinth of freedom and decisions, I am the one who defines a yes or no, and that shapes my destiny.*

*From today I freely choose to live my life to the fullest, every second every day, immersed in the eternal power of the realm of the spirit.*

*I am demon and god; I am the creator of my existence, as I want it.*

*I proclaim the time without time these decrees that transform my existence, I will fight for myself until it is possible to me and I will even try the impossible, the failure does not exist, everything is wisdom, the freedom of my soul has begun.*

Each of the six decrees contains a deep knowledge, if you meditate on them if you understand them, if you assimilate them with the reality of life, if you apply them to your life you will notice big changes, slow at the beginning, but deep in time, each decree must be read during 66 days, before to continue with the other: you will be surprised of what will happen in your mind and not toil for the appearances that you will have. When the mind is opened, the real universe is seen.

The seed generates a fragile root, to begin its growth, the leafy branches where the fruit is born, will never understand what the root does to give them life ... keep this in mind from now on.

Politicians and financiers, doctors, all make a black mass ... a black moon ritual, the same meetings where exactly the same thing happens from different points of view, dialogues, discussions, drinks, sex, orgies; etc. Concubines, bribery and others there is no difference.

In almost all the houses rituals of black masses or black moons are made, all meet to plan, to use strategies, to obtain benefits.

Today the world of Satanism is immersed in poor concepts emulating the antithesis of the church, a physical nonsense.

Meanwhile the real ones hide in their hoods in meetings where bankers dominate the world, businessmen, bankers, philanthropists, artists, etc., belong to the group.

They are who define the threads of the destiny, they are those who choose the puppet that represents them, they are who enjoy the ignorance of others who still believe in blind faith that god will come to save them or the devil in an agreement will grant to them everything.

The true Satanism is the application of the philosophy of strategy, is to create and dominate not to be dominated. All the beings can and must grow, expand, generate and create new causes, the struggle is not against god, the struggle is for the right to be free.

Religion is the refuge where the brain of slaves who rigorously follow the mandates of their oppressors is washed, it is religion that usurped the wisdom of everybody, it is religion that dominates and governs, from its hiding places.Satanism breaks that scheme, using the same laws, living in freedom, the rituals of Satanism are not made to obtain power or to subjugate the subjects, Satanism is the joint growth, it is equity, opportunity, equality, the entire respect for being free.

Every Satanist when creating its group will create the necessary rituals that must work the others, all initial group will create its own natural hierarchies, just as in nature, the wolf cub is scared away by the wolf king of the pack wolf, but the wolf alpha some day someday will dethrone it.

Start by you, generate awareness groups, demonstrate your progress with your actions, take power in your hands, build companies, negotiate, use the strategy, the options are endless, awaken in others the sense of freedom, that the employee become an entrepreneur, the servant becomes a master, the slave woman becomes the queen of her lovers, breaks the limits of submission, you already gave the first step if reached this point, now it depends on you.

Do not pursue the gold, riches are the enemy of the Satanist, dominion over nature is more valuable than gold, on doing it, won't do anything different from the crier and beggar of god.

If what you want is easy wealth, there are other forms of business.

The spiritual environment is complex, and, even more complex the social environment, therefore, the satanist navigates alone in his inner world, he is fogged in the mystery, as his personal growth, he attracts those who share the philosophy creating and generating the changes. It is important to clarify that just as in nature in the social scale, not all beings possess the same spiritual strength or are appropriate for leadership.

Each one fulfills a specific function according to his vibration, some are attracted to serve, others to create, others to work, in each area they find happiness in their actions. The satanist must take advantage of these virtues, the secret is to discover the role in which everyone feels full, to stimulate, support, guide, direct, achieve teamwork without stigmatizing or rejecting, without racism, persecution, limitations or condemnations.

The humble woman of the forest, despised by her beggar appearance, is the healer who tomorrow will save your life.

The Satanist is a leader, who knows the value of each being, he does not discriminate but takes advantage, he does not impose, he does not forces, he does not limited, he does not destroy, he does not submit, on the contrary, he discovers that he makes happy to each one and in this happiness they all triumph.

Thus the groups are created, it is not the satanic temple of the weekend, it is not the sacrifice of the gutted black cat nailed to a cross, which gives the power, power lies in the wise use of the wisdom and strategy, obtaining the greatest gain with the least effort.

In the consciousness of swarm, the slacker is the best.

Same with possessions, the effigy of the Flight of the Hummingbird delivers a judgment that all Satanists should keep in mind.

**"I do not have anything, to not be possessed by nothing"**

Every satanist starts alone, rituals are the events that allow opening spheres of wisdom, giving power, creating influences, they produce domains, itself, witchcraft rituals are the strength of the domain.

**You are selected**

With this little beginning on the philosophy, appearance, creation of Satanism, the door opens to an endless theme of the world of magic. Through different books, the complements of the different rituals are found.

Satanism, like all philosophies, is an art of knowing the laws, applying them and using them to benefit.

# RITUALS OF SATANISM

If you have reached this point I hope you have read the grimoire, otherwise you will venture into a dark and unknown universe, you will have taken the worst of the shortcuts, you will unleash energies that you will not be able to govern afterwards because you will not understand how they act, you will take the power to the darkness and in it you will succumb, nobody will be able to help you to go out, there is no how, the voices will appear uncontrolled in your mind, the invoked entities will be difficult to silence ... as a suggestion ... make a stop and read the book ... It will be of great help.

**Elements of the Satanist**
All magic event must be preceded by an attitude of conviction not of faith, the mind possesses a wall between the reason and the power, anxiety, denial, the inability to accept the possible, doubt, are elements that minimize the power.

The rituals, the rites, the prayers, the spells, the confronting of certain events will test the tenacity and spirit, where the determination and the spirit are tested, as well as the challenges and defies, are the training to gain confidence in your power, at the same time, acquiring knowledge increasing your inner strength.

Likewise or similarly, human activities in different areas of knowledge apply the same principle.

Everything requires an order, a process, demonstrative and representative elements that serve as amplifiers and support in the liberation of knowledge.

Satanism is not less; it has its mysterious identity of philosophies.

## Cape

 The cowl, very rarely named, is the hooded cape used by the ancient druids, satanists, sorcerers, philosophers, monks; etc., as all seen, this costume or dress was also adopted by the church, christened its meaning, but more than that, it was to be imposed as a symbol of devotion to god.

However, there is no difference between the satanist and the religious monk habit.

The original meaning is to be like the "shadow", to be without being, to see without being seen, to be a son of the darkness visitor of dreams.

The Satanist starts individually, the initiation is in solitary, slowly he will attract those who share his philosophy and slowly he will find with whom to share it.

*"Wherever the traces of the Master are, there the ears of the one who is ready to receive his teachings are wide-open".*

*"When the ear is able to hear, then the lips come to fill them with wisdom".*
*The Kybalion.*

It is important that all participants of a Satanist group, (all must have one or belong to one) use the hood, to show that what is important is the essence, it allows concentration, energizes the energy, that is why today great sects of politicians, merchants, bankers, use this system of mysterious and discreet meetings, nobody sees anyone, but there they are all.

# Chalice

Or sacred cup, symbol of the womb, matrix of the spells and ossuary of regrets and sorrows.

The chalice represents the creative power and the destructive power, it is opened for the adept ones and it is closed for the submissive ones.

In it is prepared the toast of water, salt, blood, wine, the communion of brotherhood.

It is important to clarify in this topic that the eucharist in Satanism is not a copy of religion, the eucharist means communion by blood, gratitude, etymologically there is no context of its origin, but... it exists about its representation in the ancient Sumerian rituals of gratitude to the gods of the underworld.

In other words, shorter, it is one the communion of the blood of those who practice the vampirism, for the striking of its execution, as well as the strength and power it releases, it was copied by the church, central ritual of the mass, which produces the greatest submission. You see the ritual, it does not participate the communion of the host and the wine, in the Catholic Eucharist is the biscuit that rewards the sinner.

In Satanism it represents the communion of blood among them.

## Elements of the altar

Every group, or individually, the Satanist must have a place to perform his sacred operation.

## A round table

In which the proclamations, the litanies are realized, the spells, the processes, the study of the subjects are created; if the group is numerous, the square is never used but they are located in a circular way.

It is the representation of the cycles, the different mutations, the negation of the hierarchies; it emphasizes equality in the creation of new teachers.

In the same way, the round table represents the universe, the cycle of life and death, the mutation of the existing thing, nobody occupies the same position, always rotate always changes, all have the same opportunities in equality.

## Stick or caduceus

Every satanist must build, create and prepare his caduceus, his own intuition tells him what signs to use, it will not only be the phallic representation complement of the chalice, but the constant reminder of power and wisdom.

Remember, all the wisdom of the universe is here and now, it vibrates in different entities that in turn vibrate in different scales, when performing these rituals, invocations, incantations and others, you will tune into some of these shadows.

## Pact of power

It must be executed during a stormy day, near midnight, remember to control your senses, as we saw in previous sections, your fear, your dread, your anxiety, all the walls of your thinking will be demolished if you really want it.

I remind you this is not a game, you are free to do it or not. It is your responsibility; the information given here is not for an obligatory execution, but information.

To make this pact, remember is a pact with the world of shadows where everything exists, you must be in total serenity, totally clean and naked, cover yourself with the habit, light two black candles, symbol of the darkness of ignorance and light of wisdom.

You must have a partner whether male or female who makes the pact, which will be done only once.

It is required that, during the Pact is done or do a toast of blood, for this, take the chalice to which water is added and a drop of blood, by the risk of contagion of different illnesses it is suggested that two persons before the pact should confirm that they are healthy.

And do not be alarmed, at Masses every eight days, they turn wine into blood, a blasphemy against life, in Satanism the blood is real.

The ritual has more power if the woman is past her second menstrual day.

After the toast, you should concentrate your attention on the shadows produced by the candles, open your mind, relax, do not think, do not wait for anything, serene your spirit, do not be attentive to anything, your mental walls will be your block, starting from that moment while the candles are consumed, if you can have some sexual activity, distract your mind.

The events, if the call has been heard, in the coming days will occur, but do not be alarmed of the form as they come. Many things can happen that obey the cause, remember you have opened a door.

If you do not feel safe, avoid reading the following sentence; sometimes just by doing so the call is made.

*Oh, lord of the terrible darkness,*
*Master, Master, of the sinister shadows*
*I am your servant, your slave, your ally*
*Give me I ask you the wished power*
*Only for some, reserved*
*Oh, master of the shadows,*
*Lord of the underworld,*
*Omnipotent power of the tombs*
*Of deceased people consumed in flames*
*I invoke you from above*
*I call you through infernal abysses*
*I call you master of masters*
*Show me clear the signs*
*I your humble servant ask you*
*To take from me, my sacred essence*
*Teach me the hidden power*
*To dominate all souls*
*Cover me with your dark coat*
*Adopt Forever my spirit*
*Take it to your ardent dwelling*
*I surrender tonight*
*To your ghastly essence*
*Accept this devotee*
*Who today consecrates you*
*Give me the magic trident*
*To trap the souls*

*Give me the power of fire*
*Show me the path of the night*
*To dominate the earthly world*
*That I have surrendered at your feet*
*Tomorrow.*

**I despise the blood of the moribund redeemer,**
**Siymbol of the misery and**
**Decline of the soul, I renounce the creeds**
**that forgiveness proclaim while their**
**dirty instincts they hide under the cassock.**

**Oh Oh lord of the shadows**
**That in the flames dance**
**Today I renounce baptism**
**Misfortune of the soul**
**Today I toast with the blood**
**That from the woman flows**
**To open my mind**
**To release my soul**
**I ask you Master**
**Give me the signs**
**You have heard**
**In the depths of the underworld**
**This proclamation**

# INITIAL RITUAL

During a stormy day, water is collected, which is mixed with black soil, before midnight, three black candles are lit in a triangle; the other lights must be off.

*When you are exfoliating your skin say mentally.*

*Sacred power of the earth*
*Immanent force of the fire*
*Aquatic mobile that merges with the wind*
*I (Say your name) invoke the supreme power*
*Dark forces of strange shadows*
*Restless spirits of black dawn*
*Hidden powers of magical presences*
*All come to this house*
*Show the path of sacred wisdom*
*The strange magic of hidden power*
*to enchant souls.*

Done with the above, contemplate the flames of the candles, avoid the anxiety and the fear with the unexpected thing, be attentive with the signals.

## Clarification

Although the desire for knowledge of the various influences that occur in the execution of rituals, these, are due to a knowledge of the seasons, the Moon, the emotional influence that produce certain elements, which affect and induce certain states, popularly known as witchcraft, are extensive topics to be treated in this Grimoire.

Each section of nature is a compendium of knowledge that are seen separately in each of the magic treatises.

Magical rituals, to which belong witchcraft and magic, are basically the same rituals that are done in Satanism, the reader is invited to consult the various grimoires, which are complement with the book of Satanism.

It is to remember that Satanism is the philosophy of witchcraft, who applies this knowledge, who discovers the implicit power, will understand the art of dominating and not being dominated.

# Universe of Magic Encyclopedia

### *Do you want to learn magic?*

Enter the school of magic through our Encyclopedia in Ophiuchus Wicca. The hidden power of the mind, the influence without space or time. A knowledge preserved for millenniums, now in your hands.

WWW.OPHIUCHUS.US

Made in the USA
Monee, IL
12 July 2021

73458851R00208